A-Z SWINDON

C000176478

Key to Map Pages	2-3
Map Pages	4-5
Large Scale Town Centre	6-37

Index
Villag
select

REFERENCE

Motorway	M4
A Road	A419
B Road	B4289
Dual Carriageway	
One-way Street Traffic flow on A Roads is indicated by a heavy line on the driver's left.	
Road Under Construction Opening dates are correct at the time of publication.	
Proposed Road	
Restricted Access	
Pedestrianized Road	
Track / Footpath	
Residential Walkway	
Railway	Heritage Station Station Level Crossing
Built-up Area	PINE CL
Local Authority Boundary	
Posttown Boundary	
Postcode Boundary (within Posttown)	
Map Continuation	28 Large Scale Town Centre 4

Car Park (selected)	P
Church or Chapel	†
Cycleway (selected)	☜
Fire Station	■
Hospital	H
House Numbers (A & B Roads only)	16 4
Information Centre	i
National Grid Reference	410
Park & Ride	Wroughton P+R
Police Station	▲
Post Office	★
Safety Camera with Speed Limit Fixed cameras and long term road works cameras. Symbols do not indicate camera direction.	30
Toilet without facilities for the Disabled with facilities for the Disabled	▽ ▽
Educational Establishment	
Hospital or Healthcare Building	
Industrial Building	
Leisure or Recreational Facility	
Place of Interest	
Public Building	
Shopping Centre or Market	
Other Selected Buildings	

SCALE

Map Pages 6-37   1:15,840

0   ¼   ½ Mile

0   250   500   750 Metres

4 inches (10.16 cm) to 1 mile   6.31 cm to 1 km

Map Pages 4-5   1:7,920

0   ⅛   ¼ Mile

0   100   200   300   400 Metres

8 inches (20.32cm) to 1 mile   12.63 cm to 1 km

A-Z Az AtoZ
— registered trade marks of
Geographers' A-Z Map Company Ltd

www./az.co.uk

EDITION 6 2015
Copyright © Geographers' A-Z Map Co. Ltd.
Telephone: 01732 781000 (Enquiries & Trade Sales)
          01732 783422 (Retail Sales)

© Crown copyright and database rights 2014 Ordnance Survey 100017302.

Safety camera information supplied by www.PocketGPSWorld.com.
Speed Camera Location Database Copyright 2014 © PocketGPSWorld.com

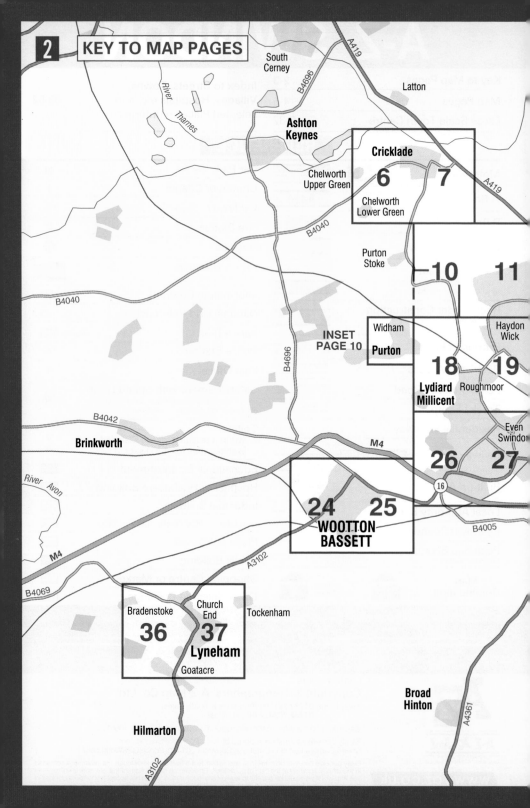

2 KEY TO MAP PAGES

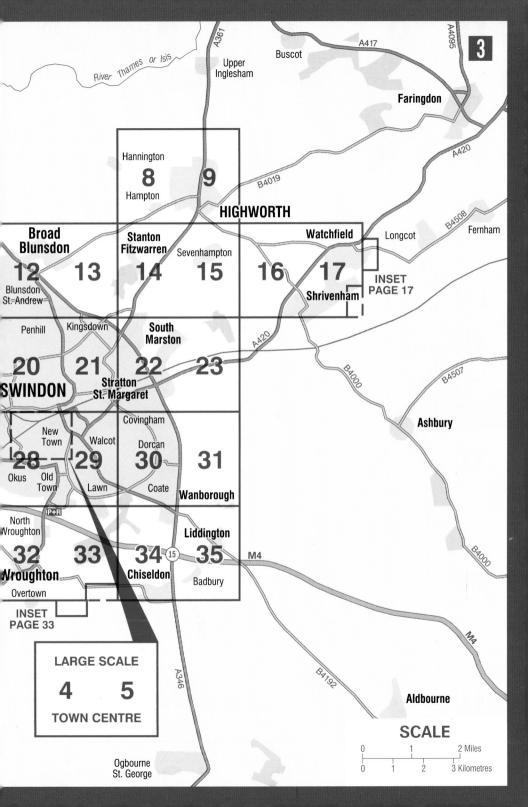

3

River Thames *or Isis*

Upper Inglesham

Buscot

A417

A4095

A361

Faringdon

A420

Hannington

8　**9**

B4019

Hampton

HIGHWORTH

A4508

Fernham

Broad Blunsdon

Stanton Fitzwarren

Sevenhampton

Watchfield

Longcot

12　**13**　**14**　**15**　**16**　**17**

INSET PAGE 17

Blunsdon St. Andrew

Shrivenham

Penhill

Kingsdown

South Marston

A420

B4000

B4507

20　**21**　**22**　**23**

SWINDON

Stratton St. Margaret

Ashbury

Covingham

New Town

Walcot

Dorcan

28　**29**　**30**　**31**

Okus

Old Town

Lawn

Coate

Wanborough

North Wroughton

P+R

Liddington

B4000

32　**33**　**34**　(15)　**35**

M4

Wroughton

Chiseldon

Badbury

Overtown

A346

INSET PAGE 33

B4192

M4

LARGE SCALE

4　**5**

TOWN CENTRE

Aldbourne

SCALE

0　　1　　2 Miles

0　1　2　3 Kilometres

Ogbourne St. George

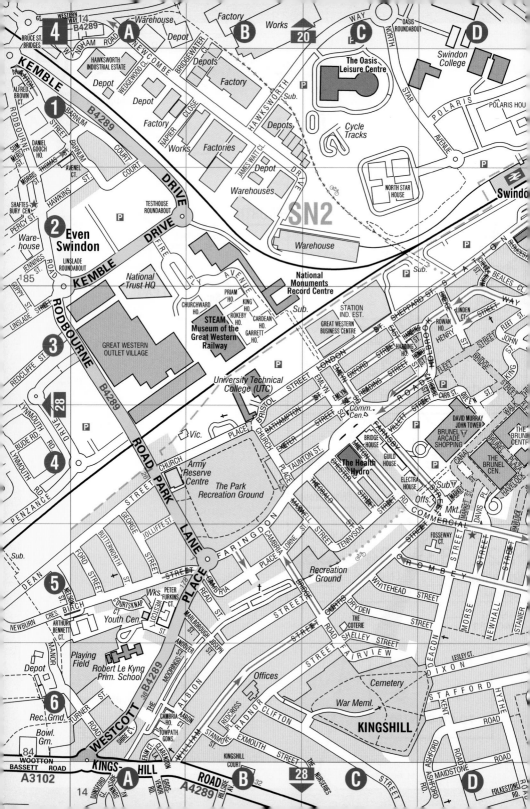

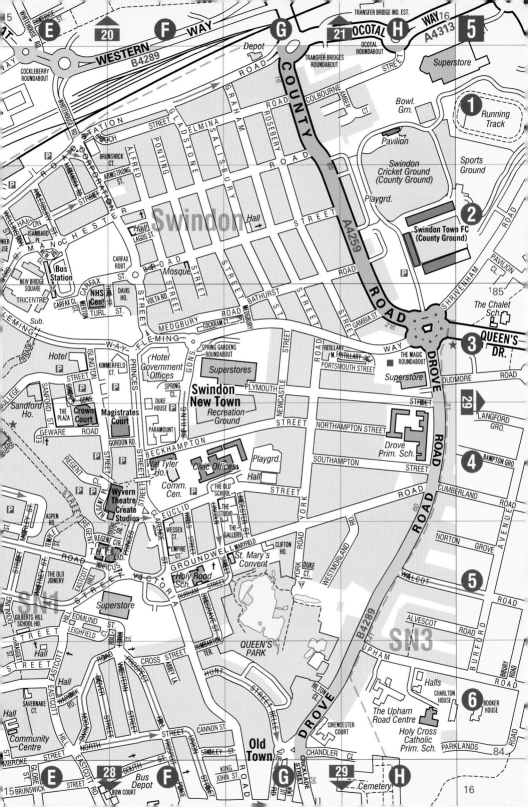

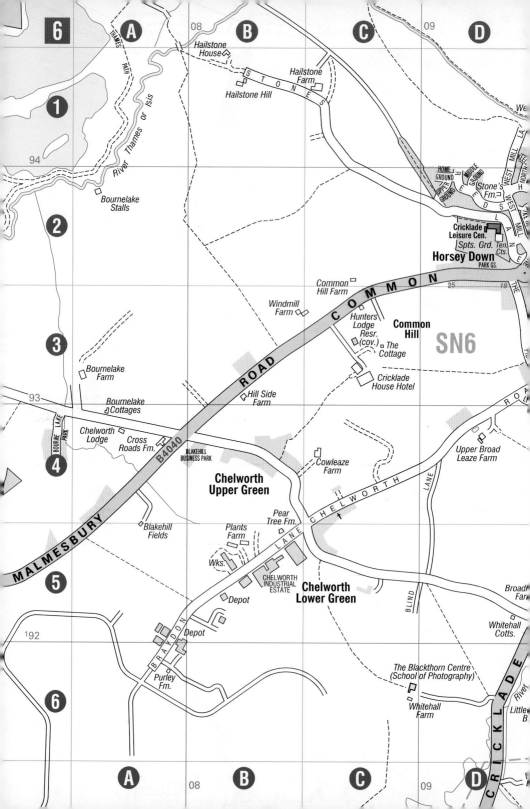

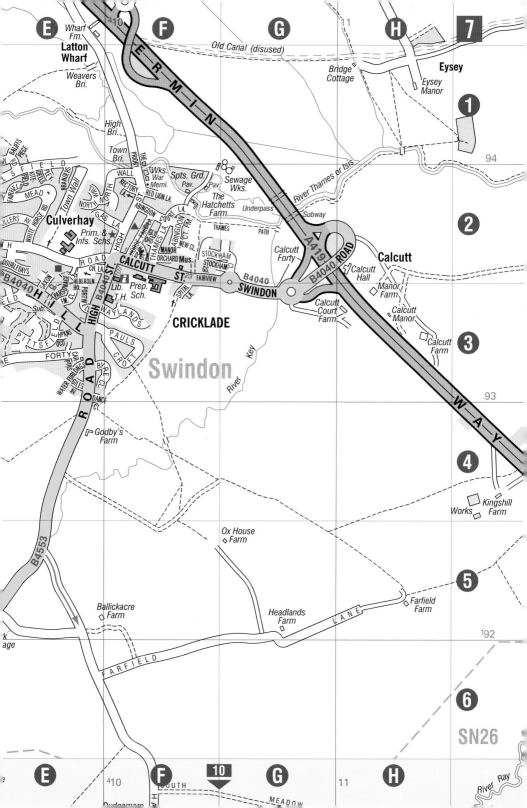

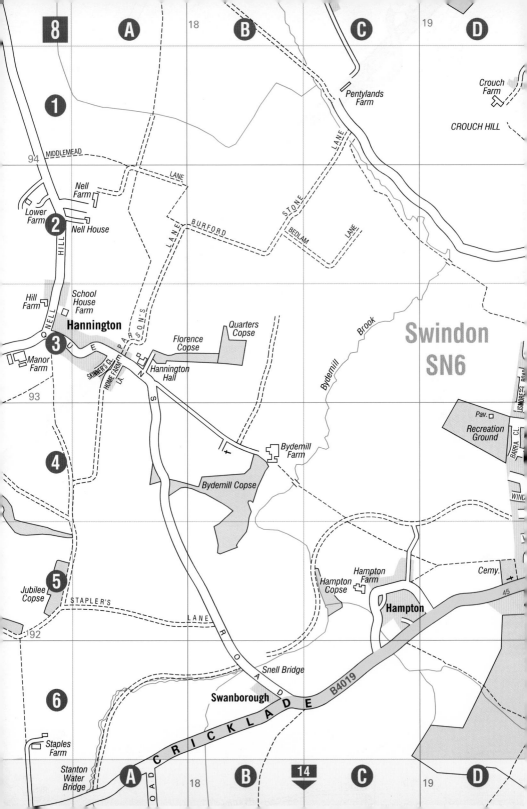

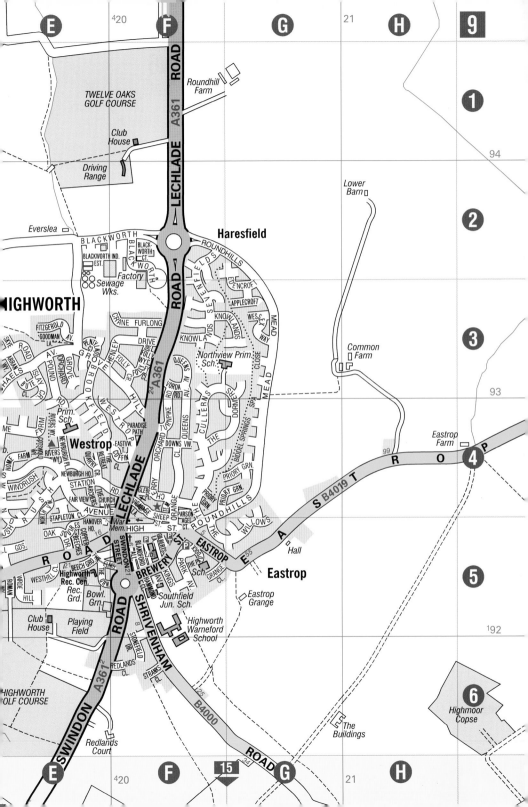

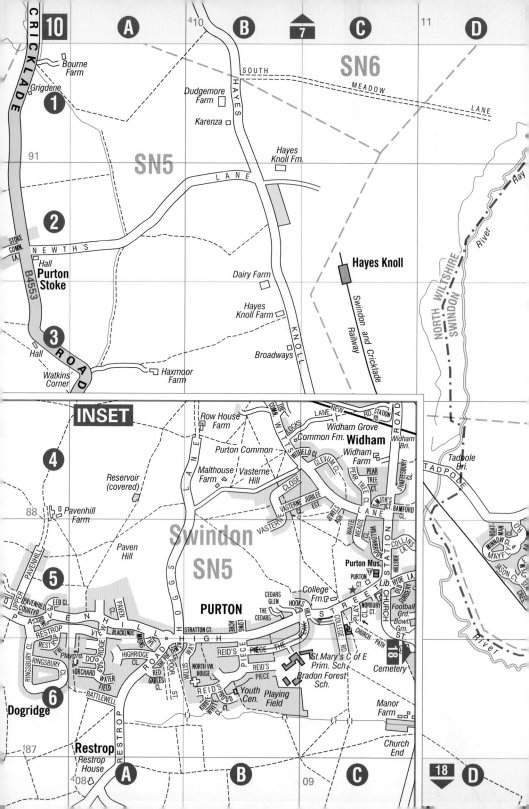

10

A   410   **B**   7   **C**   11   **D**

CRICKLADE

Bourne Farm

Grigdene

1

SN6

SOUTH

MEADOW

LANE

HAYES

Dudgemore Farm

Karenza

SN5

91

Hayes Knoll Fm.

LANE

NEWTH'S

2

STOKE COMN. LA.

Hall

Purton Stoke

Dairy Farm

B4553

ROAD

3

Hall

Watkins' Corner

Haxmoor Farm

Hayes Knoll Farm

Broadways

Hayes Knoll

Swindon and Cricklade Railway

KNOLL

River Ray

NORTH WILTSHIRE

SWINDON

INSET

4

Row House Farm

THE COMN.

NEW

LANE

RD STATION YD.

Widham Grove

Common Fm.

Widham

Widham Bri.

ROAD

WITFIELD

THE WITTS

CLOSE

Purton Common

Widham Farm

PEAR TREE CT.

SMITH'S CT.

SHAFTESBURY CL.

BAMFORD CL.

Tadpole Bri.

TADPOLE

Reservoir (covered)

Malthouse Farm

Vasterne Hill

GLEVUM CL.

PEAR TREE CL.

88

Pavenhill Farm

VASTERNE CL.

JUBILEE EST.

DEWELL

WAITE MEADS

DEWS

WILLOWBROOK

STATION

COLLINS LA.

HILLSIDE

MINNOW CL.

BOAT-MAN

MAYFLY

Paven Hill

Swindon

VASTERNE

SN5

Purton Mus.

Lib.

HYDE LA.

MAYFLY

JASON CL.

CREST

PAVENHILL

UPPER

PAVENHILL

5

FED CL.

COURTYD.

PAVENHILL

RESTROP

RESTY

Playgrd.

DOG.

ORCHARD

RINGSBURY

BLACKLNDS

GDS.

VIEW

RIDGE

PAVEN CL.

WNS.

HIGHRIDGE CL.

RED GABLES CL.

WATER FIELD

BATTLEWELL

College Fm.

THE CEDARS

HOOKS

PURTON

STRATTON CT.

LONG ACRE

CEDARS GLEN

PURTON CT.

CHURCH

CHURCH

STREET

OLD

NORBURY CT.

Football Grd. Bowl. Grn.

CHURCH PATH

HIGH

ROAD

WILLIS WAY

THE POOR

NORTH VW. HOUSE

REID'S PIECE

PIECE

REID'S PIECE

RED GABLES CL.

WHITE CL.

KIBBLE

Youth Cen.

Playing Field

St.Mary's C of E Prim. Sch.

Bradon Forest Sch.

18 Cemetery

SURGERY CL.

OLD

GRN. ST.

PLANET

RIVER

Manor Farm

6

Dogridge

RESTROP

RESTROP

187

Restrop

Restrop House

Church End

A   408   **B**   09   **C**   **18 D**

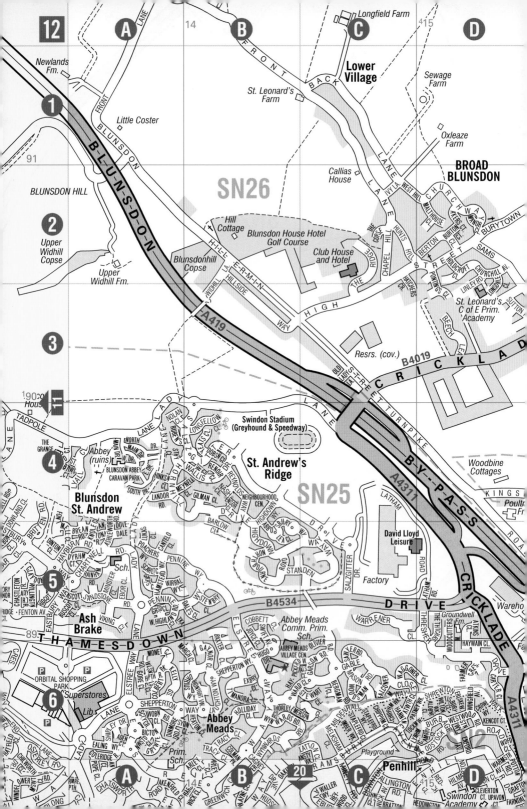

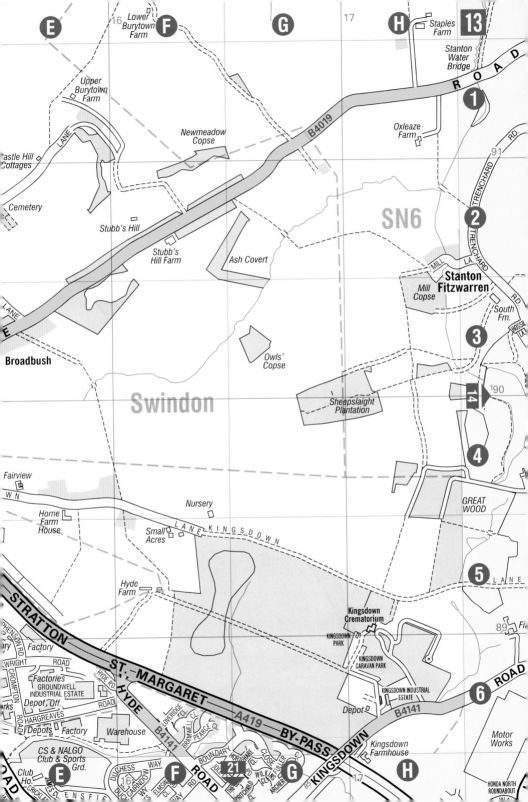

E **F** 16 *Lower Burytown Farm* **G** 17 **H** *Staples Farm* **13**

ROAD

Stanton Water Bridge

Upper Burytown Farm **1**

Castle Hill Cottages LANE *Newmeadow Copse* B4019 *Oxleaze Farm*

TRENCHARD RD. 91

Cemetery **2**

Stubb's Hill **SN6**

TRENCHARD LA. MILL LA.

Stubb's Hill Farm *Ash Covert* *Mill Copse* **Stanton Fitzwarren**

South Fm. NOSSIL LA.

LANE **3**

Broadbush *Owls' Copse* **14** 190

Swindon *Sheepslaight Plantation* **4**

GREAT WOOD

Fairview **5** LANE

WN *Nursery*

Home Farm House *Small Acres* LANE KINGSDOWN 89 Fi

Hyde Farm *Kingsdown Crematorium* **6** ROAD

STRATTON *Kingsdown Park*

Factory ROAD *Kingsdown Caravan Park*

Factories *KINGSDOWN INDUSTRIAL ESTATE*

STEPHENSON RD. CROMPTON RD. WRIGHT GROUNDWELL INDUSTRIAL ESTATE *Depot, Off.* HYDE RD. ROAD ST. MARGARET A419 BY-PASS KINGSDOWN *Depot* B4141 *Motor Works*

HARGREAVES *Depots* *Factory* *Warehouse* HYDE B4141 *Kingsdown Farmhouse*

CS & NALGO Club & Sports Grd. DUCHESS WAY LOVERIDGE CL. BRANWELL CL. PEARCE CL. BOUNDARY HORSHAM CLOSE FULLER ARCHER 85 KINGSDOWN 17 **H**

Club Ho. **E** 16 ELMSW CL. **F** ROAD **21** THE ORITCHARD WILKA CL. **G**

CRICKLAD GLENSFIE MRS CL. BUC CL CAIRNDOW WY. *HONDA NORTH ROUNDABOUT*

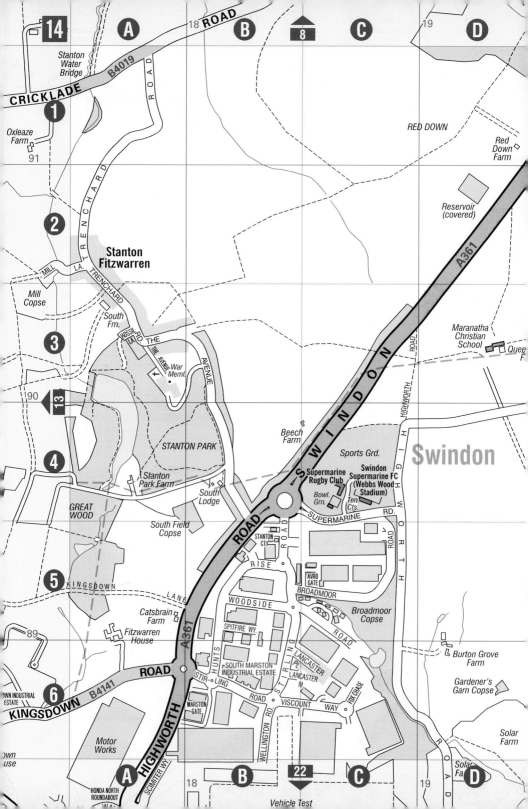

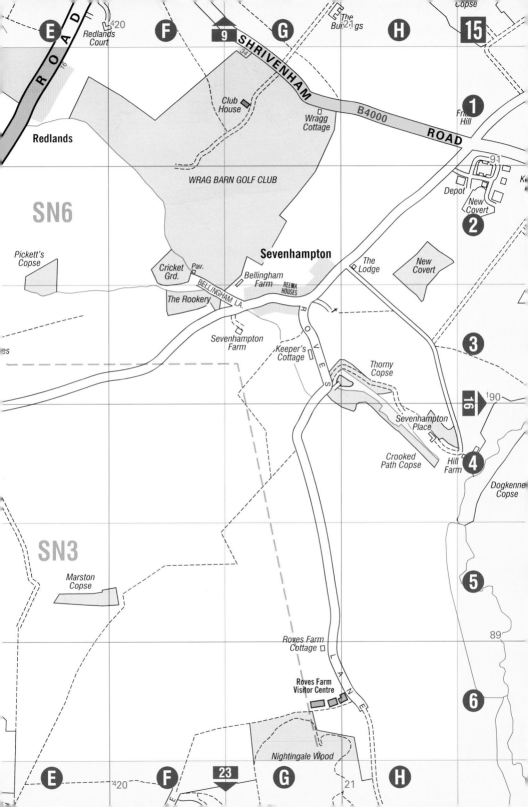

16

A   22   B   C   23   D

Highmoor Copse

1

Friars Hill

SHRIVENHAM RD.

91

B4000

Round Robin Farm

Folly Plantation

Round Robin Wood

VALE OF WHITE HORSE SWINDON

Westmill Bri.

B4508

Westmill Cotts.

Depot

New Covert

Keeper's Lodge

Westmill Farm

2

New Covert

Coombes Copse

HIGHWORTH

Little Coombes Copse

Friarsmill Bridge

Pennyhooks

3

Friars Farm

Homegrown Copse

Swan's Nest Copse

Swindon

Cole

River

15

190

ROAD

SN6

Sevenhampton Place

Hill Farm

Crooked ...th Copse

4

B4000

HIGHWORTH

Dogkennel Copse

Sandhill Farm

Sandhill Farm Cotts.

PENNYHOOKS

LANE

Hurststone Barn

5

89

STALLPITS

LANE

SAND

HI...

STALLPITS

A420

FARLEIGH RD.

DAMSON

MORTON CT.

TR...

Stallpits Farm

FORREST CL.

COLTON

CURTIS

COLTON

RD.

6

Rhyme's House

Swanhill Farm

SEND

Acorn Way

TOWN...

A   Lowerfield Wood   B   C   23   D

22

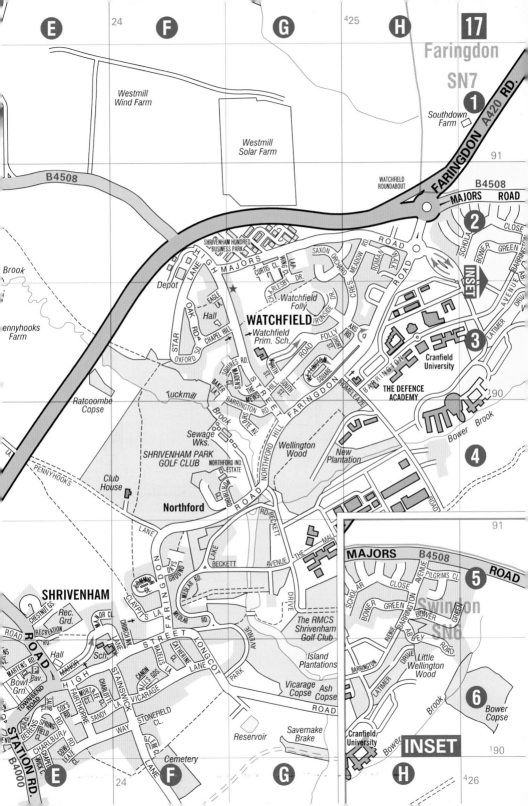

E 24 F G 425 H

1

Southdown
Farm

91

**Westmill
Wind Farm**

**Westmill
Solar Farm**

B4508

WATCHFIELD
ROUNDABOUT

B4508

MAJORS ROAD

2

FARINGDON A420 RD.

Brook

SHRIVENHAM HUNDRED
BUSINESS PARK

SAXON

ORCHARD

MEADOW

ROMAN

ROAD

ROAD

WALK

CLOSE

SCHOLA

BOWER

GREEN

AVENUE

BARRINGTON

Pennyhooks
Farm

HIGH

LANE

MAJORS

CURTIS CL.

WING LA.

CHARLESB'T

DR.

CRES.

ROAD

Depot

OAK

RD.

EAGLE
LA.

Hall

Watchfield
Folly

IRONSIDE DR.

WATCHFIELD

Watchfield
Prim. Sch.

FOLLY ST.

AXIS RD.

SHORT RD.

INSET

LATIMER

STAR

RD.

CHAPEL HILL

OXFORD SQ.

SQUARES RD.

MAIDEN'S

THE
MEWS

NORTH ST.

ST.

SOUTH ST.

ROAD

HIGHFIELD

SQUARE

HOMELEAZE

BARRINGTON

3

Cranfield
University

Ratcoombe
Copse

Tuckmill

BAKER LA.

BARRINGTON
RD.

SHUTE LA.

Brook

NORTHFORD HILL

SOUTH HILL

FARINGDON

**THE DEFENCE
ACADEMY**

190

Bower Brook

PENNYHOOKS

Sewage
Wks.

**SHRIVENHAM PARK
GOLF CLUB**

NORTHFORD IND.
ESTATE

Wellington
Wood

New
Plantation

4

Club
House

MAIN THORND
CL.

Northford

ROAD

RD.

BECKETT

91

MAJORS B4508 **ROAD**

LANE

LAKE

BECKETT

AVENUE

THE

SCHOLA

CLOSE

AVENUE

PILGRIMS CL.

5

GROUND

GAMMON
CL.

DAYS

MEDLAR LA.

MEDLAR RD.

DRIVE

BOWER

GREEN

BARRINGTON

BOWER

GREEN

**Swindon
SN6**

FARINGDON

CLAYPITS LA.

SHRIVENHAM

CHESTNUT CL.

Rec.
Grd.

MANOR CL.

CHURCH WK.

STREET

The RMCS
Shrivenham
Golf Club

Island
Plantations

AVENUE

ABBEY

ROAD

DRIVE

Little
Wellington
Wood

RECREATION
RD.

ROAD

MARTENS RD.

Hall

MANOR

HIGH

LANE

Sch.

CANON

SANDY

STAINSWICK

CATHERINE

LONGCOT

PARK

BARRINGTON

LATIMER

6

Bower
Copse

Bowl.
Grn.

Pav.

COX'S RD.

BERENS

MORT'E CT.

FAIRTHORNE

CHARLOTTE
CT.

WALLS GDS.

VICARAGE

LA.

ROAD

Vicarage
Copse

Ash
Copse

Brook

STATION RD.

B4000

CHARLBURY RD.

SPRING
FIELD CL.

CHAPEL
LANE

COW LANE

GLEBE CL.

WAY

STONEFIELD
CL.

LANE

Reservoir

Savernake
Brake

Cranfield
University

INSET

190

Cemetery

E 24 F G H 426

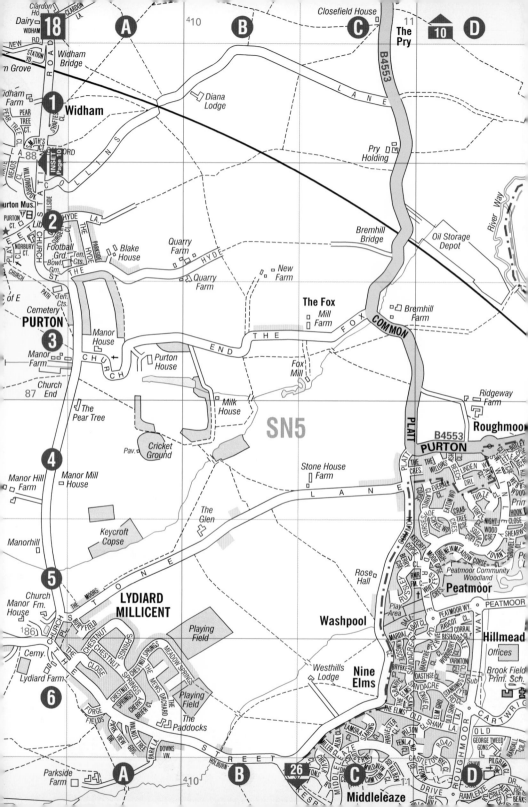

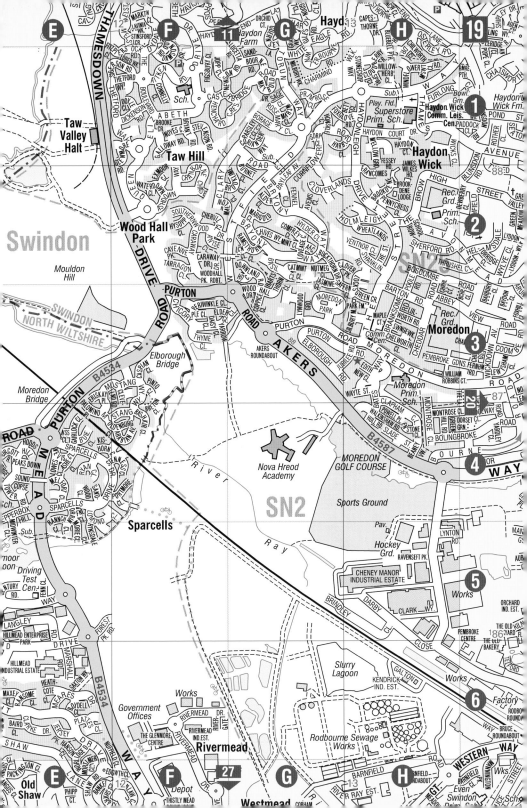

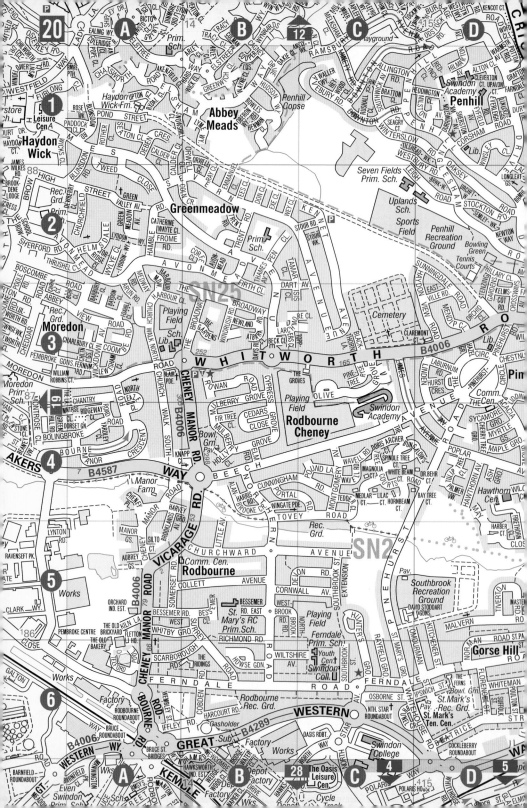

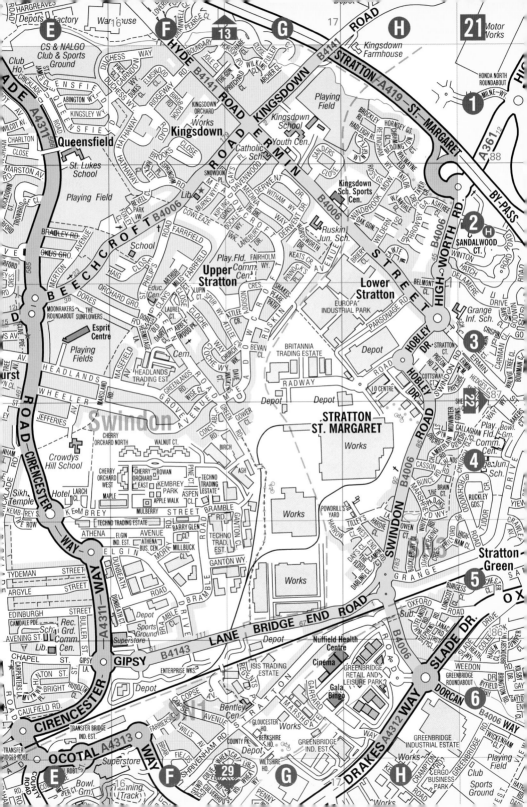

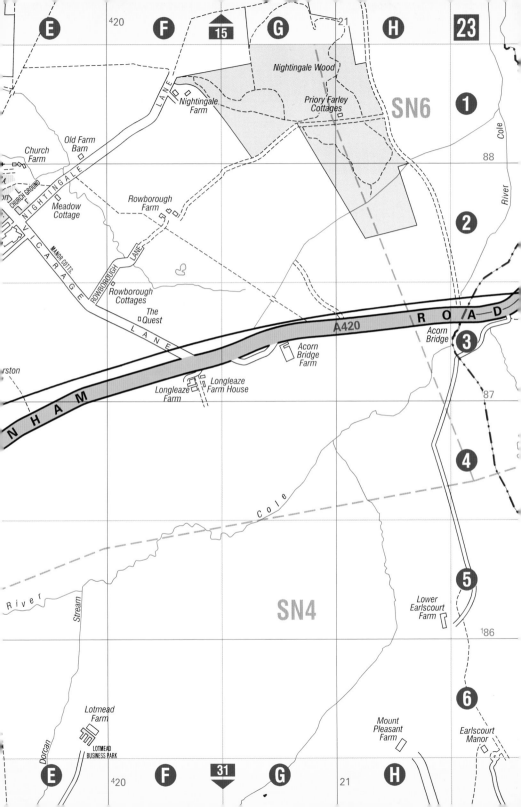

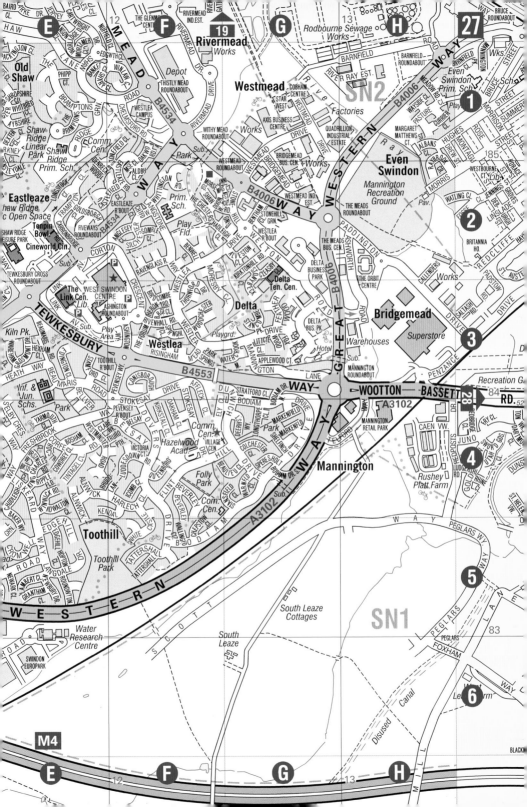

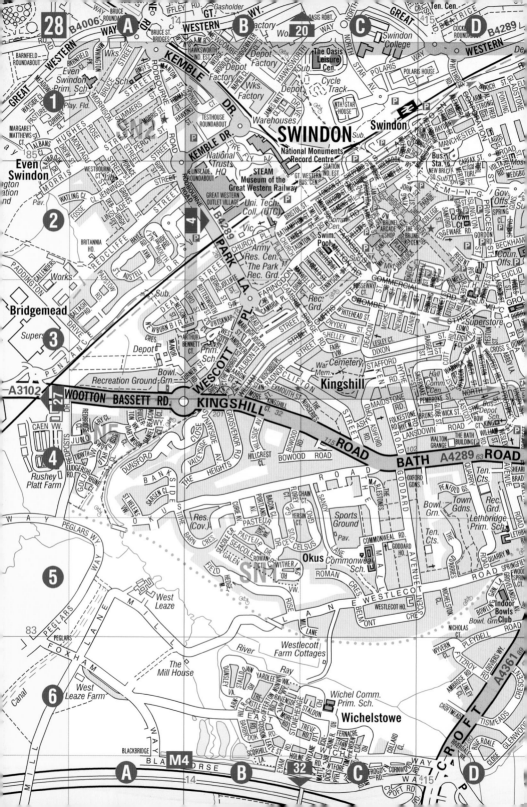

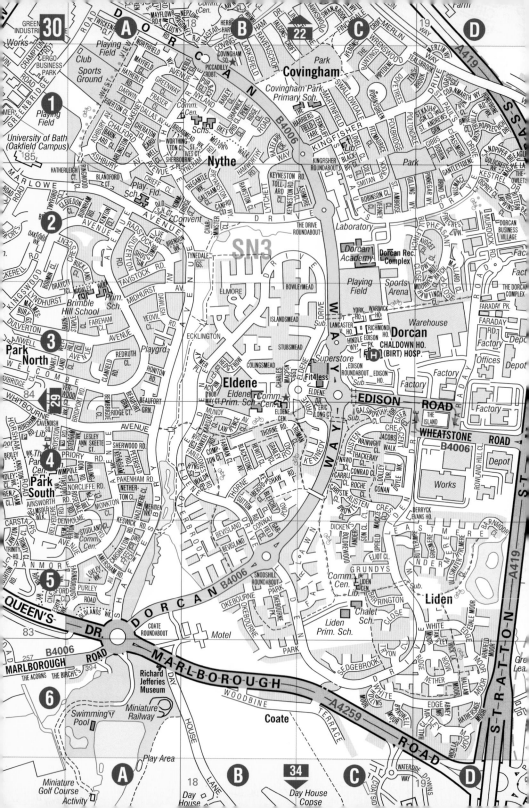

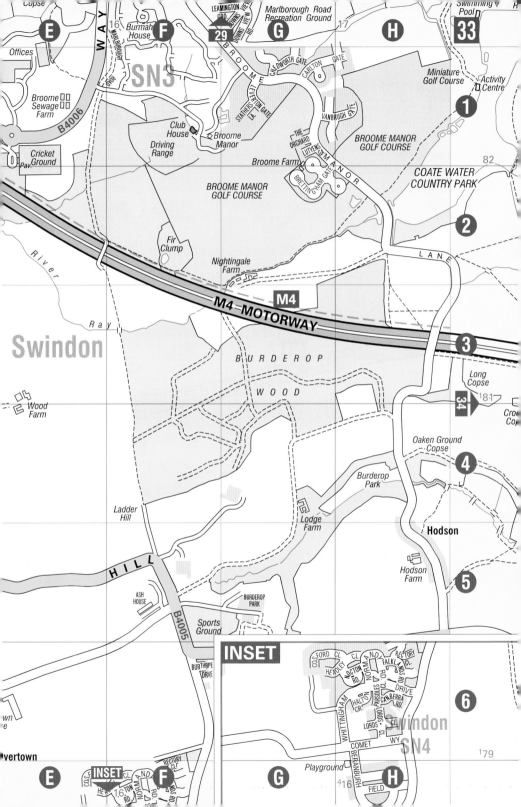

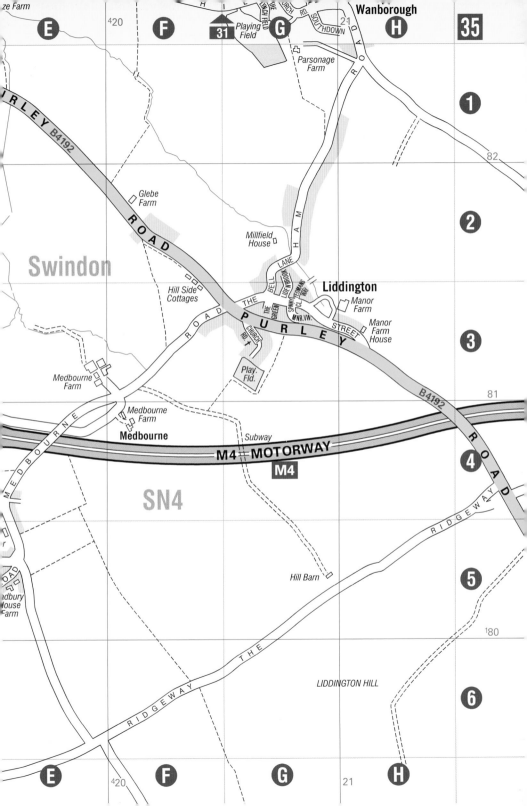

E 420 **F** **G** 31 Playing Field **H** Wanborough **35**

Parsonage Farm

1

82

Glebe Farm

2

Millfield House

Swindon

Liddington

Manor Farm

Hill Side Cottages

THE GREEN

Manor Farm House

3

ROAD

PURLEY

Medbourne Farm

CHURCH RD.

Play. Fld.

B4192

81

Medbourne Farm

Subway

4

Medbourne

M4 MOTORWAY

M4

ROAD

SN4

RIDGEWAY

adbury House Farm

Hill Barn

5

80

THE

LIDDINGTON HILL

6

RIDGEWAY

E 420 **F** **G** 21 **H**

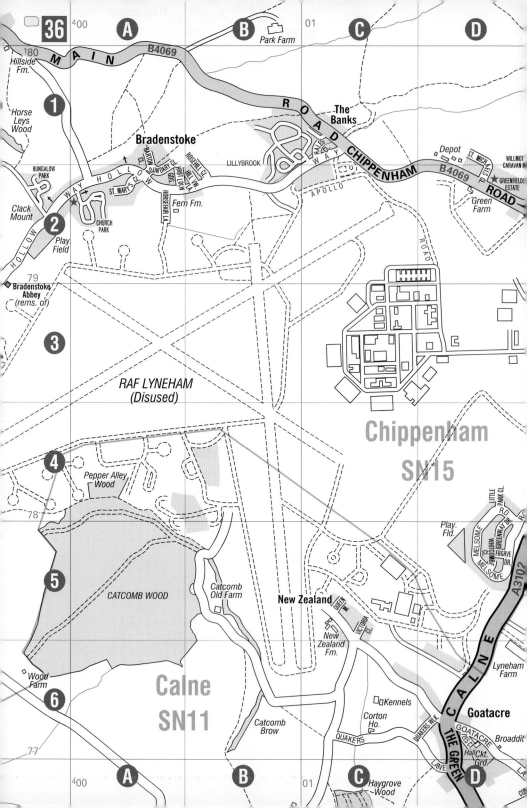

36

400   **A**   **B**   01   **C**   **D**

MAIN

B4069

Park Farm

180

1

Hillside Fm.

Horse Leys Wood

ROAD

The Banks

Bradenstoke

Depot

ST. MICHA

WILLMOT CARAVAN

BARTON CLOSE

ROSEHILL CL.

HILL VW.

LILLYBROOK

HALES WAY

ST. TO ST.

CHIPPENHAM

B4069

Greenfields Estate

GREENFIELDS ESTATE

ROAD

BUNGALOW PARK

BOUNDARY CL.

PRIORY LW.

Green Farm

HOLLOW WAY

ST. MARY'S CL.

Fern Fm.

APOLLO

2

Clack Mount

HORSEFAIR LA.

CHURCH PARK

Play. Field

ROAD

79

3

Bradenstoke Abbey (rems. of)

RAF LYNEHAM (Disused)

Chippenham SN15

4

Pepper Alley Wood

LITTLE PARK CL.

Play. Fld.

MELSOME RD.

GREENWAY DR.

WHITCOMBE DR.

TO MELSOME

FIRGROVE DR.

78

5

CATCOMB WOOD

Catcomb Old Farm

New Zealand

QUEEN

VICTORIA CL.

A3102

New Zealand Fm.

Lyneham Farm

CALNE

Wood Farm

6

Calne SN11

Kennels

Corton Ho.

Goatacre

QUAKERS WLK.

GOATACRE

Broaddit

THE GREEN

Catcomb Brow

QUAKERS

LANE

Hall Ckt. Grd.

7·7

400   **A**   **B**   01   **C**   Haygrove Wood   **D**

INDEX

Including Streets, Places & Areas, Hospitals etc., Industrial Estates,
Selected Flats & Walkways, Stations and Selected Places of Interest.

HOW TO USE THIS INDEX

1. Each street name is followed by its Postcode District, then by its Locality abbreviation(s) and then by its map reference;
e.g. **Abbey Vw. Rd.** SN25: Swin . . . .3H **19** is in the SN25 Postcode District and the Swindon Locality and is to be found in square 3H on page **19**.
The page number is shown in bold type.

2. A strict alphabetical order is followed in which Av., Rd., St., etc. (though abbreviated) are read in full and as part of the street name;
e.g. **Churchward Av.** appears after **Church Wlk. Sth.** but before **Churchward Ho.**

3. Streets and a selection of flats and walkways that cannot be shown on the mapping, appear in the index with the thoroughfare to which they are connected
shown in brackets; e.g. **Baileys Farm Gdns.** SN3: Swin . . . .2H **29** (off Buckhurst Cres.)

4. Addresses that are in more than one part are referred to as not continuous.

5. Places and areas are shown in the index in BLUE TYPE and the map reference is to the actual map square in which the town centre or area is located
and not to the place name shown on the map; e.g. **BRADENSTOKE** 2A **36**

6. An example of a selected place of interest is **Cricklade Mus.** 2F **7**

7. Examples of stations are:
Swindon Station (Rail) . . . .2D **4** (1C **28**); **Swindon Bus Station** . . . .2E **5** (1D **28**) and **Wroughton (Park & Ride)** 1D **32**

8. An example of a Hospital, Hospice or selected Healthcare facility is **GREAT WESTERN HOSPITAL** 1C **34**

9. Junction names are shown in the index in BOLD CAPITAL TYPE; e.g. **AKERS RDBT.** **3G 19**

10. Map references for entries that appear on large scale pages **4** & **5** are shown first, with small scale map references shown in brackets;
e.g. **Albion St.** SN1: Swin 6B **4** (3B **28**)

GENERAL ABBREVIATIONS

All. : Alley	**Est.** : Estate	**Nth.** : North
App. : Approach	**Fld.** : Field	**Pde.** : Parade
Arc. : Arcade	**Flds.** : Fields	**Pk.** : Park
Av. : Avenue	**Gdn.** : Garden	**Pl.** : Place
Bri. : Bridge	**Gdns.** : Gardens	**Ri.** : Rise
Bldg. : Building	**Ga.** : Gate	**Rd.** : Road
Bus. : Business	**Gt.** : Great	**Rdbt.** : Roundabout
Cvn. : Caravan	**Grn.** : Green	**Shop.** : Shopping
Cen. : Centre	**Gro.** : Grove	**Sth.** : South
Cir. : Circus	**Ho.** : House	**Sq.** : Square
Cl. : Close	**Ind.** : Industrial	**St.** : Street
Comn. : Common	**Info.** : Information	**Ter.** : Terrace
Cotts. : Cottages	**La.** : Lane	**Trad.** : Trading
Ct. : Court	**Lit.** : Little	**Va.** : Vale
Cres. : Crescent	**Mnr.** : Manor	**Vw.** : View
Cft. : Croft	**Mdw.** : Meadow	**Vis.** : Visitors
Dr. : Drive	**Mdws.** : Meadows	**Wlk.** : Walk
E. : East	**M.** : Mews	**W.** : West
Ent. : Enterprise	**Mus.** : Museum	**Yd.** : Yard

LOCALITY ABBREVIATIONS

Ash K : **Ashton Keynes**	Hook : **Hook**	Seven : **Sevenhampton**
Bad : **Badbury**	Leigh : **Leigh**	Shriv : **Shrivenham**
Blun : **Blunsdon**	Lidd : **Liddington**	S Mars : **South Marston**
Brad : **Bradenstoke**	Long : **Longcot**	Stan F : **Stanton Fitzwarren**
Burd : **Burderop**	Lyd M : **Lydiard Millicent**	Stra S : **Stratton St Margaret**
Calc : **Calcutt**	Lyd T : **Lydiard Tregoze**	Swin : **Swindon**
Chi : **Chiseldon**	Lyne : **Lyneham**	Tock : **Tockenham**
Crick : **Cricklade**	New Z : **New Zealand**	Wan : **Wanborough**
Daun L : **Dauntsey Lock**	Pres : **Preston**	Watch : **Watchfield**
Goat : **Goatacre**	Pur : **Purton**	Wid : **Widham**
Hann : **Hannington**	Pur S : **Purton Stoke**	Woot B : **Wootton Bassett**
High : **Highworth**	Rest : **Restrop**	Wro : **Wroughton**
Hod : **Hodson**		

A

	AKERS RDBT. 3G 19	**Ambrose Rd.** SN1: Swin 6D 28
	Akers Way SN2: Swin 3G 19	**Amersham Rd.** SN3: Swin 5A 30
Abbey La. SN1: Swin 6F 5 (3D 28)	**Alanbrooke Cres.** SN2: Swin 4B 20	**Amesbury Cl.** SN2: Swin 6D 12
ABBEY MEADS 6B 12	**Alba Cl.** SN5: Swin .6C 18	**Ancona Cl.** SN5: Swin 1D 26
Abbey Meads Village Cen. SN25: Swin 6B 12	**Albany Cl.** SN3: Swin 3G 29	**Anderson Cl.** SN3: Swin 5C 30
Abbey Rd. SN6: Watch 5H 17	**Albert St.** SN1: Swin 4E 29	**Andover St.** SN1: Swin 5A 4 (3B 28)
Abbey Vw. Rd. SN25: Swin 3H 19	**Albion St.** SN1: Swin 6A 4 (3B 28)	**Angelica Cl.** SN2: Swin 2G 19
Abbeywood Pk. SN2: Stra S 3F 21	**Aldborough Cl.** SN5: Swin 2F 27	**Angler Rd.** SN5: Swin 1E 27
Abbotsbury Way SN25: Swin 5B 12	**Aldbourne Cl.** SN2: Swin 6D 12	**Anglesey Cl.** SN5: Swin 2F 27
Abingdon Ct. Farm SN6: Crick 2F 7	**Alder Cl.** SN2: Swin .2G 19	**Angus Cl.** SN5: Swin 1E 27
Abingdon Ct. La. SN6: Crick 2F 7	**Alderley Rd.** SN25: Swin 5H 11	**Anise Cl.** SN2: Swin 2F 19
Abington Way SN2: Stra S 1E 21	**Alderney Cl.** SN4: Woot B 3F 25	**Ansty Wlk.** SN2: Swin 6C 12
Abney Moor SN3: Swin 6D 30	**Alexandra Rd.** SN1: Swin 2E 5 (1D 28)	**Anthony Rd.** SN4: Wro 3B 32
Acacia Gro. SN2: Swin 4D 20	**Alfred Brown Cl.** SN2: Swin 1A 4	**Antony Rd.** SN25: Swin 5A 12
Acorn Cl. SN3: Swin 3B 30	**Alfred St.** SN1: Swin 1F 5 (1D 28)	**Apollo Cl.** SN25: Swin 5E 11
Acorns, The SN3: Swin 6H 29	**Alicia Cl.** SN5: Swin 6F 11	**Apollo Rd.** SN15: Lyne 2C 36
Addinsell Rd. SN25: Swin 4H 11	**Allington Rd.** SN2: Swin 1C 20	**Apple Wlk.** SN2: Swin 4F 21
Addison Cres. SN2: Stra S 3G 21	**Allen Cl.** SN3: Swin .6F 29	**Applewood Cl.** SN5: Swin 3G 27
Aden Ct. SN25: Swin 6A 12	**Alpine Cl.** SN5: Swin 1D 26	**Aquarius Cl.** SN25: Swin 5E 11
Adwalton Cl. SN5: Swin 4E 27	**Alnwick** SN5: Swin .4E 27	**Arabian Av.** SN5: Swin 4F 19
Affleck Cl. SN5: Swin 3F 27	**Alton Cl.** SN2: Swin 1D 20	**Aragon Cl.** SN3: Swin 4H 29
Aiken Rd. SN25: Swin 1F 19	**Alvescot Rd.** SN3: Swin 5H 5 (3E 29)	**Archer Cl.** SN2: Stra S 1G 21
Ainsworth Rd. SN3: Swin 4H 29	**Alveston Cl.** SN3: Swin 2G 27	**Archers, The** SN6: High 4E 9
Akenfield Cl. SN25: Swin 1A 20	**Alwyn Cl.** SN25: Swin 5G 11	**Argosy Rd.** SN15: Lyne 4F 37
Akers Ct. SN26: Blun 2D 12	**Amber Ct.** SN1: Swin 1H 5 (1E 29)	**Argyle St.** SN2: Swin 5E 21
	Amberley Cl. SN25: Swin 2D 20	**Ariadne Rd.** SN25: Swin 5D 10

Arkwright Rd. SN25: Swin 6E **13**
Arley Cl. SN25: Swin 1B **20**
(not continuous)
Arlington Cl. SN3: Swin 1A **30**
Arliss Cl. SN25: Swin 6C **12**
Armans, The SN4: Wan 5H **31**
Armstrong St. SN1: Swin 2F **5** (1D **28**)
Arnell Cres. SN26: Swin 4H **11**
(off Addinsell Rd.)
Arnfield Moor SN3: Swin 6D **30**
Arnhem Cross SN15: Lyne 3F **37**
Arnhill Rd. SN1: Swin 6B **28**
Arnold St. SN25: Swin 5H **11**
Arran Cl. SN4: Woot B 3E **25**
Arran Way SN6: High 3E **9**
Arthur Bennett Ct.
SN1: Swin 5A **4** (3B **28**)
Arthur Miles Ct. SN2: Stra S 2F **21**
Artis Av. SN4: Wro 3C **32**
Artus Cl. SN25: Swin 5G **11**
Arundel Cl. SN3: Swin 5G **29**
Arun Rd. SN25: Swin 3A **20**
Ascham Rd. SN6: Shriv 3D **26**
Ascott Cl. SN25: Swin 5A **12**
Ash SN2: Swin 4G **21**
ASH BRAKE 5A **12**
Ashburnham Cl. SN5: Swin 4D **26**
Ashbury Av. SN3: Swin 1A **30**
Ash Cl. SN5: Swin 4D **18**
SN15: Lyne 3F **37**
Ashdown Way SN25: Swin 2F **19**
Ashen Copse Rd. SN4: Wro 3A **32**
Ashford Rd. SN1: Swin 6D **4** (4C **28**)
Ash Gdns. SN3: S Mars 2D **22**
Ash Gro. SN2: Swin 4D **20**
Ash Ho. SN4: Burd 5F **33**
Ashie Cl. SN5: Swin 4E **19**
ASHINGTON RDBT. 3F **27**
Ashington Way SN5: Swin 3F **27**
Ashkirk Cl. SN3: Swin 2F **29**
Ashlar Ct. SN3: Swin 5E **29**
Ashleworth Rd. SN25: Swin 5A **12**
Ashley Cl. SN3: Swin 2G **29**
Ashmore Cl. SN3: Swin 2C **30**
Ashridge Ct. SN25: Swin 5H **11**
Ashton Cl. SN25: Swin 5F **11**
Ashtree Cl. SN3: Stra S 2H **21**
Ashwell Cl. SN3: Swin 3G **29**
Ashworth Rd. SN5: Swin 2H **27**
Askerton Cl. SN5: Swin 6C **18**
Askew Cl. SN1: Swin 3C **26**
Aspen Cl. SN2: Swin 4F **21**
SN4: Woot B 2D **24**
Aspen Ho. SN1: Swin 4E **5**
Atbara Cl. SN25: Swin 3B **20**
Athena Av. SN2: Swin 5E **21**
Athena Bus. Cen. SN2: Swin 5F **21**
Attlee Cres. SN2: Stra S 3G **21**
Atworth Cl. SN2: Swin 6C **12**
Aubrey Gdns. SN2: Swin 5A **20**
Auden Cl. SN25: Swin 1A **20**
Audley Cl. SN3: Swin 4C **26**
Augusta Cl. SN25: Swin 5F **11**
Austen Cres. SN3: Swin 4C **30**
Avebury Rd. SN2: Swin 1C **20**
Avenel Cl. SN2: Swin 2A **4**
Avenell Rd. SN4: Wan 5G **31**
Avening St. SN2: Swin 5E **21**
Avens Cl. SN2: Swin 2G **19**
Avenue, The SN6: Stan F 3A **14**
Avenue Rd. SN1: Swin 4D **28**
Aviemore Rd. SN1: Swin 6B **28**
Avocet Cl. SN3: Swin 2D **30**
Avonmead SN25: Swin 2H **19**
Avro Gate SN3: S Mars 5C **14**
Axbridge Cl. SN3: Swin 3H **29**
Axis Bus. Cen. SN1: Swin 1G **27**
Axis Rd. SN6: Watch 3H **17**
Aylesbury St. SN1: Swin 2E **5** (1D **28**)
Aymer Pl. SN3: Swin 3B **30**
Ayrshire Cl. SN5: Swin 1E **27**
Azelin Ct. SN3: Stra S 3A **22**

B

Babington Pk. SN5: Swin 3C **26**
Back La. SN26: Blun 1C **12**
Bacon Cl. SN1: Swin 4B **28**
BADBURY 5D **34**
Badbury Rd. SN4: Bad 5D **34**
Badger Cl. SN4: Woot B 3E **25**
Badgers Cl. SN4: Wan 5H **31**
Baileys Farm Gdns. SN3: Swin 2H **29**
(off Buckhurst Cres.)
Baileys Mead SN4: Woot B 3F **25**
Baileys Way SN4: Wro 3C **32**

Bainbridge Cl. SN5: Swin 3D **26**
Baird Cl. SN5: Swin 6E **19**
Bakers Ct. SN3: Stra S 4A **22**
Bakers Fld. SN15: Lyne 2E **37**
Bakers Rd. SN4: Wro 5C **32**
Baldwin Cl. SN4: Chi 6C **34**
Bale Cl. SN5: Swin .3C **26**
Baliffs Piece SN6: Crick 1E **7**
Balmoral Cl. SN3: Swin 5H **29**
Bamford Cl. SN5: Pur 4C **10**
Bampton Gro. SN3: Swin 4H **5** (2F **29**)
Banbury Cl. SN3: Swin 5G **29**
Bancroft Cl. SN3: Swin 3C **26**
Bankfoot Cl. SN5: Swin 1E **27**
BANKS, THE 1C **36**
Bankside SN1: Swin 4A **28**
Banwell Av. SN3: Swin 3H **29**
Barbrook Rd. SN1: Swin 6B **28**
Barbury Cl. SN25: Swin 3A **20**
Barcelona Cres. SN4: Wro 3B **32**
Barcote Cl. SN25: Swin 5G **11**
Bardsey Cl. SN4: Woot B 3E **25**
Barkstead Cl. SN5: Swin 4E **27**
Barlow Cl. SN25: Swin 5B **12**
Barnard Cl. SN3: Swin 1A **30**
Barnfield Cl. SN2: Swin 1A **28**
Barnfield Rd. SN2: Swin 1H **27**
BARNFIELD RDBT. 1H **27**
Barnmoor Cl. SN5: Swin 5D **30**
Barnstaple Cl. SN3: Swin 3H **29**
Barnum Ct. SN2: Swin 1A **4** (1B **28**)
Baron Cl. SN3: Stra S 3A **22**
Barra Cl. SN6: High 4D **8**
Barrett Way SN4: Wro 4B **32**
Barrington Av. SN6: Shriv, Watch 3H **17**
Barrington Cl. SN3: Swin 5C **30**
Barrington Rd. SN6: Watch 4G **17**
Barrowby Av. SN3: Stra S 2H **21**
Barrow Cl. SN4: Woot B 4E **25**
Barry Glen Cl. SN2: Swin 5F **21**
Barton, The SN4: Woot B 3B **24**
Barton Cl. SN15: Brad 1A **36**
Barton Rd. SN25: Swin 3H **19**
Bashkir Cl. SN5: Swin 4F **19**
Basil Cl. SN3: Swin 2G **19**
Basingstoke Cl. SN5: Swin 4D **26**
Baskerville Rd. SN3: Swin 1D **30**
Bates Way SN3: Swin 3H **19**
Bathampton St. SN1: Swin 4B **4** (2B **28**)
Bath Building, The SN1: Swin 4D **28**
Bath Rd. SN1: Swin 4C **28**
SN4: Woot B 4B **24**
SN6: Crick 2E **7**
Bathurst Rd. SN1: Swin 3G **5** (2E **29**)
Battlewell SN5: Pur 6A **10**
Baxter Cl. SN5: Swin 6B **12**
Baydon Cl. SN25: Swin 3A **20**
Bayleaf Av. SN3: Swin 2G **19**
Bay Tree Ct. SN2: Swin 4D **20**
Beacon Cl. SN5: Swin 4A **28**
(off Juno Way)
Beagle Cl. SN5: Swin 5E **11**
Beales Cl. SN1: Swin 2D **4** (1C **28**)
Beamans La. SN4: Woot B 4C **24**
Beamans Pk. SN4: Woot B 4C **24**
Beaney Vw. SN2: Swin 4H **19**
Beanlands, The SN4: Wan 5G **31**
Beatrice St. SN2: Swin 1E **5** (6D **20**)
Beatty Cl. SN3: Swin 4E **29**
Beauchamp Cl. SN25: Swin 3A **20**
Beaufort Av. SN4: Woot B 5D **24**
Beaufort Grn. SN3: Swin 3A **30**
(not continuous)
Beaufort Rd. SN4: Wro 3B **32**
Beaulieu Cl. SN3: Swin 4F **27**
Beaumaris Rd. SN5: Swin 3E **27**
Beaumont Rd. SN3: Swin 2G **29**
Beck Cl. SN25: Swin 3B **20**
Beckett Av. SN3: Swin 5F **17**
Beckett Dr. SN6: Shriv 5G **17**
Beckhampton St. SN1: Swin 4F **5** (2D **28**)
Beddington Ct. SN3: Stra S 1H **21**
Bedford Rd. SN3: Swin 2G **29**
Bedlam La. SN6: Hann 2B **8**
Bedwyn Cl. SN2: Swin 3E **21**
Beech Av. SN3: Swin 4B **20**
Beechcroft Rd. SN2: Stra S 3E **21**
Beech Dr. SN5: Swin 4D **18**
Beech Gro. SN6: High 5E **9**
Beech Lea SN26: Blun 3D **12**
Beehive Cl. SN5: Swin 6D **18**
Belfast Mead SN15: Lyne 3D **37**
Belgrave St. SN1: Swin 5F **5** (3D **28**)
Belle Vue Rd. SN1: Swin 6G **5** (4E **29**)
Bell Gdns. SN3: S Mars 2D **22**
Bellingham La.
SN6: Seven 3F **15**
Bell La. SN4: Lidd .3G **35**

Bellver SN5: Swin .3E **27**
Belmont Cl. SN3: Swin 3H **21**
Belmont Cres. SN1: Swin 5C **28**
Belsay SN5: Swin 4F **27**
Belvedere Rd. SN3: Swin 5H **29**
Bembridge Cl. SN3: Swin 4A **30**
Benedict M. SN25: Swin 5F **11**
(off Tortworth Rd.)
Bennett Hill Cl. SN4: Woot B 3E **25**
Bentham Cl. SN25: Swin 2G **27**
Bentley Cl. SN3: Swin 2H **29**
Benwell Cl. SN5: Swin 2F **27**
Beranburh Fld. SN4: Wro 6H **33**
Berenger Cl. SN3: Swin 5E **29**
Berens Rd. SN6: Shriv 6E **17**
Beresford Cl. SN3: Swin 4B **30**
Bergman Cl. SN25: Swin 6C **12**
Berkeley Lawns SN3: Swin 5G **29**
Berkeley Rd. SN4: Wro 3C **32**
Berkshire Dr. SN5: Swin 1D **26**
Berkshire Ho. SN1: Swin 6G **21**
Berricot La. SN4: Bad 4D **34**
Berrington Rd. SN3: Swin 5H **29**
Berry Copse SN5: Swin 5C **18**
Berton Cl. SN26: Blun 2D **12**
Berwick Way SN2: Swin 3E **21**
Bessemer Cl. SN2: Swin 5B **20**
Bessemer Rd. E. SN2: Swin 5B **20**
Bessemer Rd. W. SN2: Swin 5A **20**
Bess Rd. SN5: Swin 4C **26**
Betjeman Av. SN4: Woot B 2D **24**
Betony Cl. SN25: Swin 1H **19**
Bevan Cl. SN2: Stra S 3G **21**
Beverley SN5: Swin 4F **27**
Beverstone Gro. SN3: Swin 4G **29**
Bevil SN5: Swin 5D **26**
Bevisland SN3: Swin 5B **30**
Bexley Wlk. SN3: Swin 4H **29**
Bibury Rd. SN3: Swin 6H **5** (3F **29**)
Bicton Rd. SN25: Swin 6A **12**
Biddel Springs SN6: High 4G **9**
Bideford Cl. SN3: Swin 3H **29**
Bilborough Dr. SN3: Swin 3G **29**
Bill Turpin Ct. SN3: Swin 4A **30**
Bincknoll La. SN4: Wro 4E **25**
Bindon Cl. SN5: Swin 3D **26**
BINKNOLL 4G **25**
Birch SN2: Swin 4F **21**
Birches, The SN3: Swin 6H **29**
Birch St. SN1: Swin 5A **4** (3A **28**)
Birchwood Rd. SN3: Stra S 4A **22**
Birdbrook Rd. SN2: Stra S 1F **21**
Birdcombe Rd. SN5: Swin 3F **27**
Birkdale Cl. SN25: Swin 5F **11**
Bishopdale Cl. SN5: Swin 5D **18**
Bishopsfield SN6: Crick 2D **6**
Bisley Cl. SN3: Swin 3H **29**
Bittern Rd. SN3: Swin 2D **30**
Blackbird Cl. SN3: Swin 1C **30**
Blackbridge SN1: Swin 6A **28**
Blackhorse Way SN1: Swin 1A **32**
Blacklands SN5: Pur 5A **10**
Blackman Gdns. SN3: Swin 5E **29**
Blackmore Cl. SN3: Swin 1D **30**
Blackstone Av. SN3: Swin 4B **30**
Blackthorn Cl. SN4: Woot B 1D **24**
Blackthorn La. SN25: Swin 3C **20**
Blackworth SN6: High 2E **9**
Blackworth Ct. SN6: High 2F **9**
Blackworth Ind. Est. SN6: High 2E **9**
Bladen Cl. SN4: Wro 4A **32**
BLAGROVE 5C **26**
Blagrove Ho. Apartments SN1: Swin 4E **29**
(off Newport St.)
Blagrove Ind. Est. SN5: Swin 6D **26**
BLAGROVE RDBT. .5C **26**
Blain Pl. SN4: Woot B 3E **25**
Blair Pde. SN25: Swin 3A **20**
Blake Cres. SN3: Swin 4B **22**
Blakehill Bus. Pk. SN6: Crick 4B **6**
Blakeney Av. SN3: Swin 1A **30**
Blakesley Cl. SN3: Swin 4G **29**
Blandford All. SN6: High 5F **9**
Blandford Cl. SN3: Swin 2A **30**
Blandford M. SN6: High 5F **9**
(off Brewery St.)
Blenheim Ct. SN4: Woot B 2E **25**
Blenheim Rd. SN3: Wro 3B **32**
Bletchley Cl. SN3: Swin 4B **30**
Blind La. SN6: Crick 5C **6**
Bloomsbury Cl. SN5: Swin 4D **26**
Bluebell Path SN25: Swin 6H **11**
Blunsdon Abbey Cvn. Pk.
SN25: Blun 4A **12**
Blunsdon Abbey Caravan Pk. SN25: Blun 4A **12**
(off Main Dr.)
Blunsdon By-Pass SN26: Blun 1A **12**
Blunsdon Hill SN26: Blun 1A **12**

Blunsdon House Hotel Golf Course—Cecil Rd.

Blunsdon House Hotel Golf Course 2B 12
Blunsdon Rd. SN25: Swin 1A 20
(not continuous)
BLUNSDON ST ANDREW 4A 12
Boatman Cl. SN25: Blun 5D 10
Bob May Ct. SN3: Swin 3B 30
Bodiam Dr. SN5: Swin 4G 27
Bodiam Dr. Nth. SN5: Swin 3G 27
Bodiam Dr. Sth. SN5: Swin 4G 27
Bodmin Cl. SN3: Swin 2H 29
Bodyhorse Hill SN4: Wan 5H 31
Boldrewood SN3: Swin 5C 30
Boleyn Cl. SN5: Swin 2D 26
Bolingbroke Rd. SN2: Swin 4H 19
Boness Rd. SN4: Wro 3B 32
Bonner Cl. SN5: Swin 3C 26
Booker Ho. SN3: Swin 6H 5 (3F 29)
Borage Cl. SN2: Swin 1G 19
Borough Flds. SN4: Woot B 3C 24
Borough Flds. Shop. Cen.
SN4: Woot B 3C 24
Boscombe Rd. SN25: Swin 2H 19
Bosham Cl. SN5: Swin 4E 27
Bosworth Rd. SN5: Swin 3D 26
Botany SN6: High 5D 8
Bothwell Rd. SN3: Swin 2G 29
Botley Copse SN5: Swin 4D 18
Boulevard, The SN25: Swin 1F 19
Boundary Cl. SN2: Stra S 1F 21
SN15: Brad 2A 36
Bourne Lake Pk. SN6: Crick 4A 6
Bourne Rd. SN2: Swin 4H 19
Bourton Av. SN3: Stra S 4A 22
Bouverie Av. SN3: Swin 5F 29
Bow Ct. SN1: Swin 6F 5 (4D 28)
Bowd's La. SN15: Lyne 1F 37
Bower Grn. SN6: Watch 5H 17
(not continuous)
Bowles Rd. SN25: Swin 1B 20
Bowleymead SN3: Swin 3B 30
Bowling Grn. La. SN1: Swin 5D 28
Bowman Cl. SN3: Stra S 3A 22
Bowman Ct. SN4: Woot B 4B 24
Bowood Rd. SN1: Swin 4B 28
Box Hedge SN4: Wan 5H 31
Boydell Cl. SN5: Swin 6E 19
Bradene Cl. SN4: Woot B 3D 24
Bradenham Rd. SN5: Swin 3D 26
BRADENSTOKE 2A 36
Bradenstoke Abbey 3A 36
Bradford Rd. SN1: Swin 4D 28
Bradley Rd. SN2: Stra S 2E 21
Bradshaw Ct. SN25: Swin 6G 11
Bradwell Moor SN3: Swin 6C 30
Braemar Cl. SN3: Swin 5G 29
Brain Ct. SN3: Stra S 4H 21
Bramble Cl. SN2: Swin 5F 21
Bramble Rd. SN2: Swin 5F 21
Bramdean Cl. *SN25: Swin* *6A 12*
(off Elstree Way)
Bramptons, The SN5: Swin 1E 27
Bramwell Cl. SN2: Swin 6F 13
Branders SN6: Crick 2E 7
Brandon Cl. SN5: Swin 3D 26
Branksome Rd. SN25: Swin 3H 19
Branscombe Dr. SN4: Woot B 4D 24
Bratton Cl. SN2: Swin 1C 20
Braxton Rd. SN25: Swin 6F 11
Braybrooke Cl. SN5: Swin 6C 18
Braydon Ct. *SN2: Swin* *1D 20*
(off Penhill Dr.)
Braydon La. SN6: Crick 6A 6
Breach La. SN4: Woot B 5A 24
Brean Rd. SN25: Swin 5A 12
Brecon Cl. SN3: Swin 6F 29
Bremhill Cl. SN2: Swin 2D 20
Brendon Wlk. SN3: Swin 2A 30
Brentfore St. SN1: Swin 1C 32
Breton Cl. SN5: Swin 4F 19
Brettingham Ga. SN3: Swin 2G 33
Brewery St. SN6: High 5F 9
Briar Flds. SN1: Swin 6F 21
Briars Cl. SN4: Woot B 2D 24
Briarswood Ct. *SN3: Swin* *5C 30*
(off Liden Dr.)
Bridge End Rd. SN3: Swin 5G 21
Bridge Ho. SN1: Swin 4C 4
Bridgelands SN4: Woot B 5C 24
Bridgeman Cl. SN3: Stra S 4A 22
BRIDGEMEAD 3H 27
Bridgemead Bus. Cen. SN5: Swin 1G 27
Bridgemead Cl. SN5: Swin 2G 27
Bridge St. SN1: Swin 3D 4 (2C 28)
(not continuous)
Bridgewater Cl. SN2: Swin 1A 4 (6B 20)
Bridport Rd. SN3: Swin 4A 30
Briery Cl. SN3: Stra S 2H 21
Bright St. SN2: Swin 6E 21
Brimble Hill SN4: Burd, Wro 5D 32
Brind Cl. SN3: Swin 2D 30
Brindley Cl. SN2: Swin 5G 19
Brington Rd. SN3: Stra S 6A 22
Bristol St. SN1: Swin 4B 4 (2B 28)
Britannia Cres. SN15: Lyne 3F 37
Britannia Ho. SN2: Swin 2A 28
Britannia Pl. SN1: Swin 4E 29
Britannia Trad. Est. SN3: Stra S 3G 21
Britten Rd. SN25: Swin 5H 11
Brixham Av. SN3: Swin 3F 29
BROAD BLUNSDON 2D 12
BROADBUSH 3E 13
Broadmead Wlk. SN3: Swin 1A 30
Broadmoor Rd. SN3: S Mars 5C 14
Broad St. SN1: Swin 2F 5 (1D 28)
Broadway, The SN25: Swin 3B 20
Brock End SN1: Swin 4E 29
Brockley Ri. SN3: Stra S 1H 21
Bromley Cl. SN3: Swin 2F 29
Bronte Cl. SN3: Swin 4C 30
Brookdene SN25: Swin 2H 19
Brookdene Lodge
SN25: Swin 2H 19
Brooke Cres. SN25: Swin 1F 19
Brooke Pl. SN4: Woot B 2E 25
Brookfield SN6: High 3E 9
Brooklands SN4: Woot B 6D 24
Brooklands Av. SN2: Swin 5A 20
Brooklime Cl. SN2: Swin 2G 19
Brookmeadow Pk. SN4: Wro 5B 32
Brooksby Way SN3: Stra S 6A 22
Brooks Cl. SN2: Stra S 1F 21
Broome Manor Golf Course 2F 33
Broome Mnr. La. SN3: Swin 6F 29
Broughton Grange SN3: Swin 4G 29
Brow, The SN25: Swin 2H 19
Browning Cl. SN3: Stra S 3A 22
BRUCE RDBT. 6A 20
Bruce St. SN2: Swin 1A 28
Bruce St. Bridges SN2: Swin 1A 4 (6A 20)
Bruddel Gro. SN3: Swin 6F 29
Brunel Arc. Shop. SN1: Swin 4D 4 (2C 28)
Brunel Centre, The SN1: Swin 4D 4 (2C 28)
Brunel Cres. SN2: Swin 6C 20
Brunel Plaza SN1: Swin 4D 4 (2C 28)
BRUNEL TREATMENT CENTRE *1C 34*
(WITHIN GREAT WESTERN HOSPITAL)
Brunswick Ct. SN1: Swin 1E 5
Brunswick St. SN1: Swin 6E 5 (4D 28)
Bruton Wlk. SN3: Swin 4H 29
Bryanston Way SN3: Swin 2B 30
Bryant Rd. SN25: Swin 1F 19
Brynards Hill SN4: Woot B 4D 24
Bryony Way SN2: Swin 2G 19
Buckhurst Cres. SN3: Swin 2H 29
Buckingham Rd. SN3: Swin 5G 29
Buckland Cl. SN3: Swin 2A 30
Bucklebury Cl. SN3: Stra S 5H 21
Buckthorn Dr. SN25: Swin 2G 19
Bude Rd. SN2: Swin 4A 4 (2A 28)
Buie Cl. SN5: Swin 4E 19
Buller St. SN2: Swin 5E 21
Bullfinch Cl. SN3: Swin 2D 30
Bunce Ct. SN5: Pur 5A 10
Bunce Rd. SN3: Stra S 4H 21
Bungalow Pk. SN15: Brad 2A 36
Bungalows, The SN2: Swin 4C 20
Buntings, The SN3: Swin 1C 30
Burbage Rd. SN2: Swin 6D 12
Burcot Cl. SN25: Swin 5F 11
Burden Cl. SN3: Stra S 5B 22
Burderop Barns SN4: Burd 6F 33
Burderop Cl. SN4: Wro 2C 32
Burderop Pk. SN4: Burd 5G 33
Burford Av. SN3: Swin 6H 5 (3F 29)
Burford Stone La. SN6: Hann 2B 8
Burgess Cl. SN3: Stra S 5A 22
Burghley Cl. SN3: Swin 2G 29
Burlongs, The SN4: Woot B 4C 24
Burnet Cl. SN2: Swin 2G 19
Burnham Rd. SN3: Swin 2A 30
Burns Way SN2: Stra S 2F 21
Burycroft SN4: Wan 4F 31
Buryfield SN5: Lyd M 5A 18
Burytown La. SN26: Blun 2D 12
Buscot Cl. SN25: Swin 5H 11
Bute Cl. SN6: High 3E 9
Buthay Ct. SN4: Woot B 3B 24
Butleigh Rd. SN25: Swin 5F 11
Buttermere SN3: Swin 5D 30
Butterworth St. SN1: Swin 5A 4 (3B 28)
Butts Bus. Cen. SN4: Chi 5C 34
Butts Rd. SN4: Chi 6C 34
Bydemill Gdns. SN6: High 5D 8
Byfield Way SN3: Stra S 6A 22
Byrd Cl. SN5: Swin 3C 26
Byre Cl. SN6: Crick 3E 7
Byron Av. SN4: Woot B 3E 25
Byron Ct. SN3: S Mars 1D 22

C

Cabot Dr. SN5: Swin 2C 26
Cadley Cl. SN2: Swin 4E 21
Caen Vw. SN5: Swin 4H 27
Caernarvon Wlk. SN3: Swin 6G 29
Cagney Dr. SN25: Swin 1B 20
Cairndow Way SN2: Stra S 1F 21
CALCUTT 2H 7
Calcutt St. SN6: Crick 2F 7
Calder Cl. SN25: Swin 1A 20
Callaghan Cl. SN3: Stra S 4A 22
Callas Hill SN4: Wan 5H 31
Callas Ri. SN4: Wan 5H 31
Callenders SN5: Swin 2H 27
Callington Rd. SN25: Swin 6E 11
Calne Rd. SN11: Goat 6D 36
SN15: Goat, Lyne 2E 37
Calstock Rd. SN25: Swin 6E 11
Calvert Rd. SN3: Swin 2F 29
Calypso Wlk. SN25: Swin 6E 11
Cambria Bri. Rd. SN1: Swin 5B 4 (3B 28)
Cambria Ho. SN1: Swin 6A 4
Cambria Pl. SN1: Swin 5B 4 (3B 28)
Cambridge Cl. SN3: Swin 5G 29
Camdale Pde. SN2: Swin 5E 21
Camden Cl. SN5: Swin 3D 26
Cameron Cl. SN3: Stra S 5H 21
Campden Rd. SN3: Swin 3F 29
Campion Ga. SN5: Swin 3C 26
Camton Rd. SN5: Swin 1C 26
Canal Wlk. SN1: Swin 4D 4 (2C 28)
Canberra Rd. SN4: Wro 6H 33
Canford Cl. SN3: Swin 2B 30
Canney, The SN4: Chi 6C 34
Canney Cl. SN4: Chi 6C 34
Cannon St. SN1: Swin 6F 5 (3D 28)
Canon Hill's Gdns. SN6: Shriv 6F 17
Cantelo Cl. SN25: Swin 5A 12
Canterbury Cl. SN3: Swin 5G 29
Capella Cres. SN25: Swin 5E 11
Capesthorne Dr. SN25: Swin 6H 11
Capitol Cl. SN3: Stra S 5C 22
Caprice Cl. SN5: Swin 1D 26
Caradon Wlk. SN25: Swin 5F 11
Caraway Dr. SN2: Swin 2F 19
Cardean Ho. SN2: Swin 3B 4
Cardigan Cl. SN3: Swin 4F 29
Cardwell Cl. SN3: Swin 1A 30
Carey Cl. SN5: Swin 3D 26
Carfax Cl. SN1: Swin 3E 5 (2D 28)
CARFAX RDBT. 2F 5
Carfax St. SN1: Swin 3E 5 (2D 28)
Carisbrook Ter. SN4: Chi 6B 34
Carlisle Av. SN3: Swin 5E 29
Carlton Ga. SN3: Swin 1G 33
Carman Cl. SN3: Stra S 3A 22
Carmel Wlk. *SN3: Swin* *3G 29*
(off Woodhouse Rd.)
Carpenters SN6: Crick 3E 7
Carpenters La. SN2: Swin 6E 21
Carrington Gdns. SN4: Woot B 1D 24
Carroll Cl. SN3: Swin 4C 30
Carronbridge Rd. SN5: Swin 2E 27
Carr St. SN1: Swin 3D 4 (2C 28)
Carshalton Rd. SN3: Swin 5A 30
Carstairs Av. SN3: Swin 5H 29
Carter Cl. SN25: Swin 6D 12
Cartwright Dr. SN5: Swin 6D 18
Carver Cl. SN3: Stra S 4B 22
Caspian Cl. SN5: Swin 3F 19
Cassini Dr. SN25: Swin 5E 11
Casson Rd. SN3: Stra S 4H 21
Casterbridge Rd. SN25: Swin 1F 19
Castilian M. SN5: Swin 1D 26
Castle Dore SN5: Swin 3D 26
Castlefield Cl. SN5: Swin 2E 27
Castleton Rd. SN5: Swin 1D 26
Castle Vw. SN4: Chi 6C 34
Castle Vw. Rd. SN3: Stra S 5B 22
Catherine Cl. SN6: Shriv 6F 17
Catherine St. SN1: Swin 3D 4 (2C 28)
Catherine Wayte Cl. SN25: Swin 2A 20
Catmint Cl. SN2: Swin 2G 19
Caulfield Rd. SN2: Swin 6E 21
Cavendish Sq. SN3: Swin 4H 29
Caversham Cl. SN3: Swin 3G 29
Cavie Cl. SN5: Swin 6D 18
Cawte M. SN3: Stra S 2H 21
Caxton Cl. SN3: Swin 4G 29
Caxton Ct. *SN3: Swin* *4G 29*
(off Caxton Cl.)
Cayenne Pk. SN2: Swin 2F 19
Cecil Rd. SN3: Swin 2H 29

Cedars, The SN5: Pur 5B 10
Cedars Cl. SN2: Swin 4B 20
Cedars Glen SN5: Pur 5B 10
Celcus Gro. SN1: Swin 5B 28
Central Trad. Est. SN3: Swin 5E 29
Centurion Way SN1: Stra S 6B 22
Century Rd. SN5: Swin 5E 19
Chain Cl. SN1: Swin 4C 28
Chalford Av. SN3: Swin 1A 30
Chalgrove Fld. SN5: Swin 5D 26
Chalvedon Grn. SN3: Swin 3G 29
(off Bilborough Dr.)
Chamberlain Rd. SN3: Stra S 4H 21
Chancellor Cl. SN5: Swin 2C 26
Chandler Cl. SN1: Swin 6S 5 (3E 29)
Chandos Cl. SN2: Swin 2D 26
Chantry Rd. SN2: Swin 3A 20
Chapel Hill SN6: Watch 3F 17
SN26: Blun 2C 12
Chapel La. SN3: S Mars 1D 22
SN4: Wan 5H 31
Chapel Orchard SN4: Wan 5H 31
Chapel St. SN2: Swin 6E 21
Chapelwick Cl. SN6: Shriv 6E 17
Charfield Cl. SN3: Swin 4H 29
Charlbury Cl. SN25: Swin 3A 20
Charlbury Rd. SN6: Shriv 6E 17
Charlesby Dr. SN6: Watch 3G 17
Charles Macpherson Gdns.
SN3: Swin 3B 30
Charlock Path SN25: Swin 1H 19
(off Capesthorne Dr.)
Charlotte Cl. SN6: Shriv 6E 17
Charlotte M. SN1: Swin 4E 29
Charlton Cl. SN2: Swin 1E 21
Charlton Ho. SN3: Swin 6H 5 (3E 29)
Charmind Wlk. SN25: Swin 1G 19
Charminster Cl. SN3: Swin 2B 30
Charolais Dr. SN5: Swin 1D 26
Charterhouse Rd. SN4: Wro 4A 32
Chartley Grn. SN5: Swin 3D 26
Chartwell Rd. SN5: Swin 5A 12
Chase Wood SN5: Swin 5D 18
Chastleton Rd. SN25: Swin 5H 11
Chatsworth Rd. SN25: Swin 1A 20
Chaucer Cl. SN4: Woot B 2D 24
Cheddar Rd. SN25: Swin 3H 19
Chedworth Ga. SN3: Swin 1G 33
Chelmsford Rd. SN1: Swin 1F 27
Chelworth Cl. SN25: Swin 3H 19
Chelworth Ind. Est. SN6: Crick 5B 6
CHELWORTH LOWER GREEN 5C 6
Chelworth Rd. SN6: Crick 4C 6
CHELWORTH UPPER GREEN 4B 6
Cheney Mnr. Ind. Est. SN2: Swin 5H 19
Cheney Mnr. Rd. SN2: Swin 6A 20
(Ferndale Rd.)
SN2: Swin 3B 20
(Whitworth Rd.)
Cheney Pl. SN2: Swin 4A 20
Chepstow Cl. SN5: Swin 5F 27
Cheraton Cl. SN3: Swin 1A 30
Cherbury Wlk. SN3: Swin 2H 29
Cherhill Ct. SN25: Swin 3H 19
Cherry Brier Cl. SN5: Lyd M 6A 18
Cherry Orchard SN6: High 4F 9
Cherry Orchard E. SN2: Swin 4F 21
Cherry Orchard Nth. SN2: Swin 4E 21
Cherry Orchard W. SN2: Swin 4E 21
Cherry Tree Gro. SN2: Swin 4D 20
Cherry Tree Rd. SN6: Crick 2D 6
Chervil Cl. SN2: Swin 2F 19
Chesford Cl. SN3: Swin 5H 29
Chesterfield Cl. SN5: Swin 2F 27
Chesters, The SN5: Swin 2F 27
Chester St. SN1: Swin 4C 4 (2C 28)
Chestnut Av. SN2: Swin 3D 20
Chestnut Gdns. SN6: Shriv 5E 17
Chestnut Springs SN5: Lyd M 6A 18
Chevalier Cl. SN5: Swin 1C 26
Cheviot Cl. SN5: Swin 2D 26
Chickerell Rd. SN3: Swin 2H 29
Chicory Cl. SN2: Swin 3F 19
Chilworth Cl. SN25: Swin 1H 19
Chippenham Cl. SN2: Swin 6C 12
Chippenham Rd. SN15: Lyne 1C 36
Chippenham Wlk. SN2: Swin 6C 12
CHISELDON 6C 34
Chiseldon Ct. SN4: Chi 6C 34
Chives Way SN2: Swin 2G 19
Chobham Cl. SN3: Stra S 1H 21
Chopin M. SN2: Swin 6G 11
Christie Cl. SN3: Swin 4C 30
Chudleigh SN5: Swin 4E 27
CHURCH END 3E 37
Church End SN5: Pur 3A 18

Church End Cl. SN15: Lyne 3E 37
Church Farm La. SN3: S Mars 2D 22
Church Farm M. SN15: Lyne 3E 37
Churchfield SN25: Swin 2A 20
Church Ground SN3: S Mars 2E 23
Church Hill SN4: Wro 5A 32
Church Hill Cl. SN4: Woot B 2F 25
Churchill Av. SN26: Blun 2D 12
Church La. SN6: Crick 2E 7
SN15: Lyne 3F 37
Church Pk. SN15: Brad 2A 36
Church Path SN5: Pur 5C 10
Church Pl. SN1: Swin 4A 4 (2B 28)
SN5: Lyd M 5A 18
Church Rd. SN1: Swin 4E 29
SN4: Lidd 3G 35
SN4: Wan 6G 31
Church St. SN3: Stra S 3A 22
SN4: Chi 6C 34
SN4: Woot B .3B 24
SN5: Pur 5C 10
Church Vw. SN6: High 4E 9
Church Wlk. SN2: Stra S 3G 21
SN6: Shriv 5F 17
Church Wlk. Nth. SN25: Swin 3A 20
Church Wlk. Sth. SN25: Swin 3A 20
Churchward Av. SN2: Swin 5B 20
Churchward Ho. SN2: Swin 3B 4
Church Way SN3: Stra S 4A 22
Churchway SN26: Blun 2D 12
Cineworld Cinema
Swindon, Whitehill Way 2E 27
Circle, The SN5: Swin 3D 20
Cirencester Cl. SN1: Swin 6G 5 (3E 29)
Cirencester Way SN2: Swin 4E 21
Clanfield Rd. SN3: Swin 3A 30
Clapham Cl. SN2: Swin 4H 19
Claremont Cl. SN25: Swin 3C 20
Clarence St. SN1: Swin 4F 5 (3D 28)
Clarendon Dr. SN4: Woot B 4D 24
Clarendon La. SN1: Swin 6A 4 (3B 28)
Clare Wlk. SN5: Swin 4E 27
Clarke Dr. SN5: Swin 6E 19
Clary Rd. SN2: Swin 2F 19
Claydon St. SN25: Swin 5H 11
Clayhill Copse SN5: Swin 4D 18
Claypits La. SN6: Shriv 5F 17
Clays Cl. SN2: Stra S 3F 21
Clearwater Bus. Pk. SN5: Swin 5D 26
Cleasby Cl. SN5: Swin 2G 27
Cleeve Lawns SN3: Swin 5G 29
Clementine Rd. SN25: Blun, Swin 5D 10
Clevedon Cl. SN3: Swin 2H 29
Cleveland Rd. SN5: Swin 3F 19
Cleverton Ct. SN2: Swin 1D 20
Cleves Cl. SN5: Swin 2D 26
Cleycourt Rd. SN6: Shriv 6D 16
Cliffords SN6: Crick 2E 7
Clifton Ho. SN1: Swin 5G 5
Clifton St. SN1: Swin 6B 4 (3B 28)
Clinton Cl. SN3: Swin 4C 26
Clive Pde. SN2: Swin 3E 21
Cloatley Cres. SN4: Woot B 5D 24
Cloche Way SN3: Stra S 3F 21
Close, The SN5: Lyd M 6A 18
Cloudberry Rd. SN25: Swin 1H 19
Clouts Wood SN5: Swin 4D 18
Cloverlands SN25: Swin 2G 19
Clover Pk. SN25: Swin 2H 19
Clyde Cotts. SN4: Wro 2C 32
Clydesdale Cl. SN5: Swin 1D 26
COATE 6B 30
COATE RDBT. 5A 30
Coate Water Country Pk. 1A 34
Coatside Way SN3: Swin 1C 34
Cobbett Cl. SN25: Swin 5B 12
Cobbett Ct. SN6: High 5F 9
(off Hammond Cl.)
Cobden Rd. SN2: Swin 6B 20
Cobham Cen. SN5: Swin 1G 27
COCKLEBERRY RDBT. 1E 5 (6D 20)
Cockram Ct. SN1: Swin 3F 5
Coffin Cl. SN6: High 4F 9
Colbert Pk. SN2: Swin 6A 12
Colbourne St. SN1: Swin 1G 5 (1E 29)
Colchester Cl. SN5: Swin 4G 27
Colebrook Rd. SN3: Stra S 6A 22
Cole Cl. SN3: Swin 2C 30
Coleridge Cl. SN4: Woot B 2D 24
Coleridge Rd. SN25: Swin 6A 12
Colingsmead SN3: Swin 3B 30
Collard Cl. SN1: Swin 6C 28
College Ct. SN1: Swin 5E 5
(off Regent Cir.)
College Grn. SN4: Wan 5G 31
College Rd. SN5: Pur 5C 10
College St. SN1: Swin 3E 5 (2D 28)
Collett Av. SN2: Swin 5B 20

Collins La. SN5: Pur 5C 10
Colman Pk. SN25: Swin 6B 12
Coln Cres. SN25: Swin 2B 20
Colston Cl. SN3: Swin 4H 29
Colton Rd. SN6: Shriv 6D 16
Combe La. SN11: Goat 6D 36
Comet Cl. SN15: Lyne 3F 37
Comet Way SN4: Wro 6H 33
Comfrey Cl. SN2: Swin 2G 19
Commercial Rd. SN1: Swin 4D 4 (2C 28)
Common, The SN5: Pur 4B 10
Common Cl. SN6: Shriv 5F 17
COMMON HEAD RDBT. 1D 34
COMMON HILL 3C 6
Common Rd. SN6: Crick 3C 6
Common Platt SN5: Pur, Swin 3C 18
Commonweal Rd. SN1: Swin 5C 28
Compton Cl. SN3: Swin 4B 30
Conan Doyle Wlk. SN3: Swin 4C 30
Concord Wlk. SN3: Swin 3G 29
(off Rutland Dr.)
Conisborough SN5: Swin 3F 27
Connelly Cl. SN3: Swin 1F 19
Conrad Cl. SN3: Swin 4C 30
Constable Rd. SN2: Swin 4F 21
Constantine Cl. SN3: Stra S 6C 22
Conway Rd. SN3: Swin 5B 30
Conyers Cl. SN5: Swin 4C 26
Cookham Rd. SN25: Swin 5F 11
Coombe Cl. SN4: Wro 5D 32
Coombe Rd. SN3: Swin 3A 20
Copeer Flds. SN25: Swin 1B 20
Coped Hall Bus. Pk. SN4: Woot B 1E 25
Coped Hall Bus Pk. SN4: Woot B 2E 25
COPED HALL RDBT. 1E 25
Copper Beeches SN6: High 5E 9
Copperfields SN25: Swin 6G 11
Coppice Cl. SN3: Swin 3G 19
Copse, The SN26: Blun 2C 12
Copse Av. SN1: Swin 6F 21
Corby Av. SN3: Swin 5F 29
Corfe Cl. SN25: Swin 2B 20
Corfe Rd. SN5: Swin 4E 27
Coriander Way SN2: Swin 1G 19
Corinium Way SN3: Stra S 6B 22
Cornflower Rd. SN25: Swin 2G 19
Cornmarsh Way SN3: Swin 1D 30
Cornwall Av. SN2: Swin 5B 20
Cornwood Rd. SN1: Swin 1C 32
Coronation Rd. SN4: Wro 4B 32
Corporation St. SN1: Swin 1E 5 (1D 28)
Corral Cl. SN5: Swin 5D 18
Corsham Rd. SN3: Swin 1D 20
Corton Cres. SN5: Swin 2E 27
Cosdon Rd. SN1: Swin 6B 28
Cosford Cl. SN4: Wro 6G 33
Coterie, The SN1: Swin 5C 4
Cotswold Way SN6: High 4E 9
Cottars Cl. SN3: Stra S 3A 22
Cottington Cl. SN5: Swin 4D 26
Cottsway Cl. SN3: Stra S 3H 21
Council Houses SN4: Tock 4E 5
County Ground 2H 5 (1E 29)
County Pk. SN1: Swin 6G 21
County Rd. SN1: Swin 1G 5 (1E 29)
Courtenay Rd. SN3: Swin 2H 29
Courtsknap Cl. SN1: Swin 5A 4 (3B 28)
Coventry Cl. SN4: Wro 3C 32
COVINGHAM 1B 30
Covingham Dr. SN3: Swin 6B 22
Covingham Sq. SN3: Swin 1B 30
Cowdrey Cl. SN5: Swin 4E 27
Cowleaze Cl. SN6: Shriv 6E 17
Cowleaze Cres. SN4: Wro 4A 32
Cowleaze Wlk. SN2: Stra S 2F 21
Cowley Wlk. SN3: Swin 3A 30
Cox's Rd. SN6: Shriv 6E 17
Coxstalls SN4: Woot B 3C 24
Crabtree Copse SN5: Swin 4D 18
Crampton Rd. SN3: Swin 1H 29
Cranborne Chase SN25: Swin 2F 19
Crane Furlong SN6: High 3F 9
Cranfield University 3H 11
Cranmore Av. SN3: Swin 4H 29
Crawford Cl. SN5: Swin 4D 26
Crawley Av. SN3: Stra S 5A 22
Create Studios 4F 5
Crescent, The SN5: Swin 4D 18
CRICKLADE 2F 7
Cricklade Ct. SN1: Swin 4E 29
(off Cricklade St.)
Cricklade Leisure Cen. 2D 6
Cricklade Mus. 2F 7
Cricklade Rd. SN2: Stra S 1E 21
SN2: Swin 5D 12
SN5: Pur S, Wid 6D 6
SN6: Blun, High, Stan F 3C 12
SN6: Crick, Pur S 6D 6

Cricklade Rd.—Elms, The

Cricklade Rd. SN25: Swin 5D 12
SN26: Blun 3C 12
Cricklade St. SN1: Swin 6G 5 (4E 29)
Crieff Cl. SN3: Swin 2A 30
Criollo Pl. *SN5: Swin* *4F 19*
(off Mustang Way)
Crispin Cl. SN3: Stra S 3A 22
Croft Gallery, The *4E 29*
(off Devizes Rd.)
Croft Ho. *SN3: Swin* *6A 22*
(off Twickenham Cl.)
Croftmead SN1: Swin 6D 28
Croft Rd. SN1: Swin 1D 32
(not continuous)
Croft Sports Cen. 5E 29
Crombey St. SN1: Swin 5C 4 (3C 28)
Cromer Ct. *SN3: Swin* *5C 30*
(off Liden Dr.)
Crompton Rd. SN25: Swin 6E 13
Cromwell SN5: Swin 5E 27
Croome Cl. SN25: Swin 4E 11
Crosby Wlk. SN3: Swin 5H 29
Cross St. SN1: Swin 6F 5 (3D 28)
Crossways Av. SN25: Swin 3D 20
Crosswood Rd. SN3: Swin 5H 29
Crown Court
Swindon 4E 5 (2D 28)
Crudwell Way SN2: Swin 6D 12
Cuckoo's Mead *SN3: Swin* *2D 30*
(off Magpie La.)
Culbone Rd. SN1: Swin 6C 28
Cullerne Rd. SN3: Stra S 5B 22
Cullerns, The SN6: High 4F 9
Culpepper Cl. SN3: Swin 4H 29
CULVERHAY 2E 7
Culverhouse Rd. SN1: Swin 1F 29
Cumberland Rd. SN3: Swin 4H 5 (2F 29)
Cunetio Rd. SN3: Stra S 6B 22
Cunningham Rd. SN2: Swin 4B 20
Curie Av. SN1: Swin 4B 28
Curnicks, The SN4: Chi 6B 34
Curtis Cl. SN6: Watch 2G 17
Curtis Rd. SN6: Shriv 6D 16
Curtis St. SN1: Swin 5C 4 (3C 28)
Cypress Gro. SN2: Swin 3B 20

D

Dacre Rd. SN3: Swin 2H 29
Daisy Brook SN4: Woot B 4D 24
Daisy Cl. SN2: Swin 3F 19
Dalefoot Cl. SN5: Swin 5C 18
Dales Cl. SN25: Swin 5B 12
Dallas Av. SN3: Swin 1A 30
Dalton Cl. SN3: Swin 1G 29
Dalwood Cl. SN3: Swin 5A 30
Dammas La. SN1: Swin 4E 29
Damson Cres. SN25: Swin 1F 19
Damson Path *SN25: Swin* *1F 19*
(off Damson Cres.)
Damson Trees SN6: Shriv 6D 16
Dance Ct. SN6: Crick 3E 7
Danestone Cl. SN5: Swin 1C 26
Daniel Cl. SN5: Swin 4A 28
Daniel Gooch Ho. SN2: Swin 1A 4
Daniels Ct. *SN4: Chi* *6C 34*
(off Dewey Cl.)
Darby Cl. SN2: Swin 5H 19
Darcey Cl. SN5: Swin 2C 26
Darius Way SN25: Swin 6B 12
Darling Cl. SN3: Stra S 5H 21
Darnley Cl. SN3: Swin 2G 29
Dart Av. SN25: Swin 3B 20
Dartmoor Cl. SN5: Swin 4A 28
Darwin Cl. SN3: Swin 1A 30
Davenham Cl. SN3: Swin 5H 29
Davenwood SN2: Stra S 2G 21
Dave Watkins Ct. SN2: Stra S 3G 21
David Lloyd Leisure
Swindon 5C 12
David Murray John Tower SN1: Swin 4D 4 (2C 28)
David Stoddart Gdns. SN2: Swin 5D 20
Da Vinci Wlk. SN4: Woot B 5D 24
Davis Ho. SN1: Swin 3F 5
Davis Pl. SN1: Swin 4D 4
Dawlish Rd. SN3: Swin 3A 30
Day Ho. La. SN3: Swin 6A 30
SN4: Swin 6A 30
Day's Cl. SN3: Stra S 5H 21
Days Ground SN6: Shriv 5F 17
Days Ri. SN25: Swin 3B 20
Deacon St. SN1: Swin 6D 4 (3C 28)
Deansfield SN6: Crick 3E 7
Dean St. SN1: Swin 5A 4 (3A 28)
Dearden Wlk. SN3: Swin 6F 29
Deben Cres. SN25: Swin 1A 20
Deburgh St. SN2: Swin 2A 28
Deerhurst Way SN5: Swin 4G 27
Defence Academy, The 3H 17
Delamere Dr. SN3: Stra S 2A 22
Delft Cres. SN25: Swin 5G 11
Delius Cl. SN25: Swin 4H 11
DELTA 2G 27
Delta Bus. Pk. SN5: Swin 3G 27
(not continuous)
Delta Tennis Cen. 2G 27
Denbeck Wood SN5: Swin 2E 27
Denbigh Cl. SN3: Swin 5F 29
Denby Rd. SN25: Swin 5H 11
Deneb Dr. SN25: Swin 5E 11
Denholme Rd. SN3: Swin 5H 29
Denton Ct. SN3: Stra S 4A 22
Derby Ct. *SN3: Swin* *2F 29*
(off Lennox Dr.)
Derryck Evans Ho. SN3: Swin 4D 30
Derwent Dr. SN2: Stra S 2G 21
(not continuous)
Desborough SN5: Swin 5D 26
Deva Cl. SN3: Stra S 6C 22
Devereux Cl. SN5: Swin 3C 26
Devizes Rd. SN1: Swin 4E 29
SN4: Wro 4C 32
Devon Rd. SN2: Swin 5B 20
Dewberry Cl. SN25: Swin 2A 20
Dewell M. SN3: Swin 5E 29
Dewey Cl. SN4: Chi 6C 34
Dexter Cl. SN5: Swin 1E 27
Dickens Cl. SN3: Swin 5C 30
Dickenson Rd. SN25: Swin 1F 19
Dickson Rd. SN15: Lyne 4E 37
Dingle, The SN4: Wan 5G 31
Dinmore Rd. SN25: Swin 6A 12
Dinton Cl. SN25: Swin 5H 11
Dione Cres. SN25: Swin 5E 11
Dior Dr. SN4: Woot B 5D 24
Divinity Cl. SN4: Wan 5H 31
Dixon St. SN1: Swin 6D 4 (3C 28)
Dixon Way SN5: Swin 2F 27
Dobbin Cl. SN3: Swin 1D 30
Dobson Cl. SN25: Swin 4B 12
Dockle Way SN2: Stra S 2G 21
DOGRIDGE 6A 10
Dogridge SN5: Pur 6A 10
Dolina Rd. SN25: Swin 6G 11
Don Cl. SN25: Swin 2B 20
Donnington Gro. SN3: Swin 4G 29
DORCAN 3C 30
Dorcan Bus. Village SN3: Swin 2D 30
Dorcan Complex, The SN3: Swin 3D 30
Dorcan Recreation Complex 2C 30
Dorcan Way SN3: Swin 6A 22
Dorchester Rd. SN3: Swin 5G 29
Dores Ct. SN2: Stra S 3F 21
Dores Rd. SN2: Stra S 3E 21
Doris Archer Ct. SN2: Swin 4C 20
Dormers, The SN6: High 4F 9
Dorney Rd. SN25: Swin 4F 11
Dorset Grn. SN2: Swin 4A 20
Doubledays SN6: Crick 2E 7
Douglas Rd. SN3: Swin 2G 29
Doulton Cl. SN25: Swin 5G 11
Dovedale SN25: Swin 5A 12
Dover St. SN1: Swin 6E 5 (3D 28)
Dovetrees SN3: Swin 1C 30
Dowlais Cl. SN25: Swin 6F 11
Dowland Cl. SN25: Swin 4H 11
Dowling St. SN1: Swin 5E 5 (3D 28)
Downland Rd. SN2: Swin 2G 19
Downs Rd. SN4: Chi 6D 34
Downs Vw. SN4: Woot B 4C 24
SN5: Lyd M 6A 18
SN6: High 4F 9
Downs Vw. Rd. SN3: Swin 6G 29
Downs Way SN3: Swin 1D 34
Downton Rd. SN2: Swin 1C 20
Doyle Cl. SN25: Swin 1F 19
Dragonfly Rd. SN3: Stra S 6A 22
Drakes Mdw. SN3: Swin 1G 29
DRAKES RDBT. 2F 29
Drakes Way SN3: Swin 2F 29
(not continuous)
Draycott Cl. SN3: Swin 3H 29
Draycott Rd. SN4: Chi 6B 34
Draymans Ct. SN4: Woot B 5C 24
Drayton Wlk. SN3: Swin 2G 29
Dr Behr Ct. SN2: Swin 4D 20
Drew St. SN2: Swin 1H 27
Drive, The SN3: Swin 1A 30
SN4: Woot B 6A 24
Drive Rdbt., The SN3: Swin 2C 30
Drove Rd. SN1: Swin 3H 5 (3E 29)
Dryden Pl. SN4: Woot B 2E 25
Dryden St. SN1: Swin 5C 4 (3C 28)
Duchess Way SN2: Stra S 1E 21
Dudley Rd. SN3: Swin 2G 29
Dudmore Rd. SN3: Swin 3H 5 (2F 29)
Duke Ho. SN1: Swin 3F 5
Dukes Cl. SN2: Stra S 1F 21
Dulverton Av. SN3: Swin 3H 29
Dumbarton Ter. SN1: Swin 6F 5 (3D 28)
Dunbar Rd. SN4: Wro 3B 32
Dunbeath Ct. SN2: Swin 5F 21
Dunbeath Rd. SN2: Swin 5F 21
Dunley Cl. SN25: Swin 5G 11
Dunnington Rd. SN4: Woot B 5C 24
Dunraven Cl. SN3: Swin 4G 29
Dunsford Cl. SN1: Swin 6A 4 (4A 28)
Dunsley Va. SN1: Swin 6B 28
Dunster Cl. SN3: Swin 5F 29
Dunvant Rd. SN25: Swin 5F 11
Dunwich Dr. SN5: Swin 3G 27
Durham St. SN1: Swin 5F 5 (3D 28)
Durnford Rd. SN2: Swin 1D 20
Durrington Wlk. SN2: Swin 1D 20
Dussek Pl. SN25: Swin 5H 11
Dydale Rd. SN25: Swin 6F 11
(not continuous)
Dykes M. SN4: Chi 6C 34
Dyrham Ct. SN25: Swin 5A 12
Dyson Rd. SN25: Swin 4H 11

E

Eagle Cl. SN3: Swin 1D 30
Eagle La. SN6: Watch 3F 17
Ealing Way SN25: Swin 6A 12
Earl Cl. SN5: Swin 1C 26
Eastbury Way SN25: Swin 5G 11
Eastcott Hill SN1: Swin 6E 5 (3D 28)
(not continuous)
Eastcott Rd. SN1: Swin 6E 5 (4D 28)
East Dr. SN25: Blun 4A 12
Eastern Av. SN3: Swin 2F 29
EASTLEAZE 2F 27
Eastleaze Rd. SN5: Swin 2F 27
EASTLEAZE RDBT. 2F 27
Eastmere SN3: Swin 5C 30
EASTROP 5F 9
Eastrop SN6: High 5F 9
East St. SN1: Swin 3C 4 (2C 28)
Eastview Ter. SN6: High 4F 9
Eastville Rd. SN25: Swin 3D 20
E. Wichel Way SN1: Swin 6B 28
Eastwood Av. SN4: Woot B 4D 24
Eaton Cl. SN3: Swin 5H 29
Eaton Wood SN5: Swin 4D 18
Ebor Cl. SN25: Swin 5A 12
Eccleston Cl. SN3: Swin 5A 30
Ecklington SN3: Swin 3B 30
Edale Moor SN3: Swin 5D 30
Eddleston Rd. SN1: Swin 1F 29
Edencroft SN6: High 3G 9
Edgar Row Cl. SN4: Wro 4B 32
Edgehill SN5: Swin 5E 27
Edgeware Rd. SN1: Swin 4E 5 (2D 28)
Edgeworth Cl. SN5: Swin 1F 27
Edinburgh St. SN2: Swin 5E 21
Edington Cl. SN5: Swin 3E 27
Edison Ho. SN3: Swin 3C 30
Edison Pk. SN3: Swin 3C 30
Edison Rd. SN3: Swin 3C 30
EDISON RDBT. 3C 30
Edith New Cl. SN2: Swin 3H 19
Edmund St. SN1: Swin 5E 5 (3D 28)
Egdon Cl. SN25: Swin 6G 11
Egerton Cl. SN3: Swin 1A 30
Eider Av. SN15: Lyne 4E 37
Elborough Rd. SN2: Swin 3G 19
Elcombe Av. SN4: Wro 4A 32
ELDENE 3B 30
Eldene Cen. SN3: Swin 4B 30
Eldene Dr. SN3: Swin 4B 30
Elder Cl. SN2: Swin 3F 19
Eldred Wlk. SN25: Swin 1F 19
Electra Ho. SN1: Swin 4C 4
Elgar Cl. SN25: Swin 5H 11
Elgin Dr. SN2: Swin 5F 21
Elgin Ind. Est. SN2: Swin 5F 21
Eliot Cl. SN3: Swin 5C 30
Elizabeth Ho. SN3: Swin 2G 29
Ellendune Shop. Cen. SN4: Wro 4B 32
Ellingdon Rd. SN4: Wro 3A 32
Elm Cl. SN4: Woot B 1D 24
SN15: Lyne 3G 37
Elm Ct. SN4: Woot B 4C 24
Elm Gro. SN5: Swin 6D 18
Elmina Rd. SN1: Swin 1F 5 (1D 28)
Elmore SN3: Swin 3B 30
Elm Pk. SN4: Woot B 4C 24
Elm Rd. SN2: Swin 4B 20
Elms, The SN5: Swin 6C 18
SN6: High 5E 9

42 A-Z Swindon

Elmswood Cl. SN2: Stra S 1F 21
Elsham Way SN25: Swin 1A 20
Elsie Hazel Ct. SN5: Swin 4D 26
Elstree Way SN25: Swin 6A 12
Elver Cl. SN3: Stra S 6A 22
Ely Cl. SN5: Swin .4F 27
Ely Ct. SN4: Wro .5B 32
EMBANKMENT RDBT. 5E 29
Emerson Cl. SN25: Swin 6B 12
Emlyn Sq. SN1: Swin 3C 4 (2C 28)
Emmanuel Cl. SN25: Swin 2B 20
Empire Cinema
  Swindon, Greenbridge 6G 21
Empire Ct. SN1: Swin 5F 5
Endeavour Rd. SN3: Stra S 6A 22
Enford Av. SN2: Swin 6D 12
Englefield SN4: Woot B 4D 24
Ensor Cl. SN25: Swin 4B 12
Enstone Cl. SN2: Swin 4H 19
Enterprise Works SN2: Swin 6F 21
Ergo Bus. Pk. SN3: Swin 1H 29
Eric Long Ct. SN3: Swin 4C 30
Erin Ct. SN1: Swin 6A 4 (3B 28)
Eriskay Pl. SN5: Swin 3E 19
Erlestoke Way SN2: Swin 6D 12
Ermin M. SN3: Stra S 3A 22
Ermin St. SN2: Stra S 1G 21
  SN3: Stra S 3A 22
  SN26: Blun 2B 12
Ermin Way SN6: Calc, Crick 1F 7
Eshton Wlk. SN3: Swin 5H 29
Espringham Ho. SN2: Stra S 2F 21
  (off Hathaway Rd.)
Espringham Pl. SN2: Stra S 2F 21
Esprit Centre 3E 21
Essex Wlk. SN3: Swin 6C 28
Estella Cl. SN25: Swin 6G 11
Euclid St. SN1: Swin 4F 5 (2D 28)
Europa Ind. Pk. SN3: Stra S 3G 21
Europark SN5: Swin 6C 26
Euroway SN5: Swin 6C 26
Eveleigh Rd. SN4: Woot B 3D 24
Evelyn St. SN2: Swin 5E 29
EVEN SWINDON 2A 4 (1H 27)
Evergreens Cl. SN3: Swin 5B 22
Everleigh Rd. SN2: Swin 1D 20
Ewden Cl. SN25: Swin 3C 28
Eworth Cl. SN5: Swin 3C 26
Exbury Cl. SN25: Swin 6B 12
Exe Cl. SN25: Swin 2B 20
Exeter St. SN1: Swin 4B 4 (2B 28)
Exmoor Cl. SN25: Swin 2F 19
Exmouth St. SN1: Swin 6B 4 (3B 28)
Eyam Rd. SN25: Swin 1B 32
Eyre Cl. SN25: Swin 6F 11
EYSEY 1H 7

F

Fairfax Cl. SN3: Swin 1G 29
Fairfield SN4: Woot B 2D 24
  SN6: Crick 2E 7
Fairford Cres. SN3: Swin 2E 21
Fairholm Way SN2: Stra S 2G 21
Fairlawn SN3: Swin 5C 30
Fairthorne Way SN6: Shriv 6E 17
Fair Vw. SN6: High 4E 9
Fairview SN1: Swin 6C 4 (3C 28)
  SN6: Crick 2F 7
Fairwater Ct. SN4: Wro 5B 32
Falconer M. SN25: Swin 6C 12
Falconscroft SN3: Swin 3B 22
Falkirk Rd. SN4: Wro 3B 32
Falklands Rd. SN4: Wro 6H 33
Falmouth Gro. SN3: Swin 4F 29
Fanstones Rd. SN3: Swin 4B 30
Faraday Pk. SN3: Swin 3D 30
Faraday Rd. SN3: Swin 4D 30
Fareham Cl. SN3: Swin 3A 30
Farfield La. SN6: Crick 6F 7
Faringdon Rd. SN1: Swin 5B 4 (3B 28)
  SN6: Shriv 5F 17
  SN6: Watch 4G 17
  SN7: Long, Watch 2H 17
Farleigh Cres. SN3: Swin 5F 29
Farleigh Rd. SN6: Shriv 6D 16
Farman Cl. SN3: Swin 1C 30
Farmer Cres. SN25: Swin 6D 12
Farmhouse La. SN1: Swin 1F 29
Farnborough Rd. SN3: Swin 5A 30
Farndale Cl. SN2: Swin 1D 20
Farne Way SN4: Woot B 3F 25
Farnsby St. SN1: Swin 4C 4 (2C 28)
Farrfield SN2: Stra S 2F 21
Farriers Cl. SN1: Swin 6F 21
Farthing La. SN15: Lyne 1E 37
Fawley Cl. SN25: Swin 4F 11

Feather Wood SN5: Swin 3G 27
Fenby Pl. SN25: Swin 5G 11
Fenland Cl. SN5: Swin 6C 18
Fenn Cl. SN5: Swin 5E 19
Fennel Cl. SN2: Swin 2G 19
Fenton Av. SN25: Swin 5H 11
Fernacre Rd. SN1: Swin 6C 28
Ferndale Rd. SN2: Swin 6A 20
Fernham Rd. SN25: Swin 3A 20
Ferns, The SN2: Swin 6D 20
Ferrers Dr. SN5: Swin 4C 26
Fessey Ho. SN1: Swin 1H 19
Fiddle, The SN6: Crick 3D 6
Fieldfare SN3: Swin 1C 30
Field Ri. SN1: Swin 5B 28
Fields, The SN3: Stra S 5H 21
Figsbury Cl. SN25: Swin 1F 19
Filsham Rd. SN25: Swin 5F 11
Finchdale SN3: Swin 6C 22
Firecrest Vw. SN3: Swin 2D 30
Fire Fly Av. SN2: Swin 2A 4 (1B 28)
Firethorn Cl. SN3: Swin 5D 20
Firth Cl. SN25: Swin 3B 20
Fir Tree Cl. SN2: Swin 4B 20
Fit4less
  Swindon 3C 30
Fitkin Cl. SN5: Swin 5G 11
Fitwell Rd. SN25: Swin 5F 11
Fitzgerald Av. SN6: High 3E 9
Fitzmaurice Cl. SN3: Swin 1C 30
Fitzpiers Cl. SN25: Swin 1F 19
Fitzroy Rd. SN1: Swin 6D 28
FIVEWAYS RDBT. 2E 27
Fleet St. SN1: Swin 3D 4 (2C 28)
Fleetwood Cl. SN5: Swin 5D 26
Fleming Way SN1: Swin 3E 5 (2D 28)
Fletton Ho. SN2: Swin 5A 20
Flint Hill SN5: Swin 4F 27
Florence St. SN1: Swin 6D 28
Florey Cl. SN1: Swin 4B 28
Folkestone Rd. SN1: Swin 6D 4 (4C 28)
Folly Cl. SN6: High 3F 9
Folly Cres. SN6: High 3F 9
  SN6: Watch 3G 17
Folly Dr. SN6: High 3F 9
Folly Way SN6: High 3F 9
Fonthill Wlk. SN3: Swin 3F 29
Fontmell Cl. SN3: Swin 4H 11
Ford St. SN1: Swin 5A 4 (3B 28)
Forester Cl. SN3: Swin 4C 30
Forest Pk. Rd. SN5: Swin 5E 19
Forge Flds. SN5: Lyd M 6A 18
Forrest Cl. SN6: Shriv 6D 16
Forsey Cl. SN3: Swin 1D 30
Forty, The SN6: Crick 3E 7
Forum, The SN5: Swin 3F 27
Forum Cl. SN3: Stra S 6B 22
Fosse Cl. SN3: Swin 2A 28
Fosseway Ct. SN1: Swin 5D 4 (3C 28)
Foundry Ri. SN4: Chi 6C 34
Fovant Cl. SN5: Swin 5D 18
Fowey SN5: Swin 5D 26
FOX, THE 3C 18
Fox, The SN5: Pur .3B 18
Foxbridge SN3: Swin 1C 30
Fox Brook SN4: Woot B 3E 25
Foxglove Rd. SN25: Swin 1G 19
Foxham Way SN1: Swin 6A 28
Foxhill Cl. SN25: Swin 3A 20
Foxleaze SN6: Crick 1E 7
Foxley Cl. SN2: Stra S 2F 21
Fox Wood SN5: Swin 3G 27
Frampton Cl. SN5: Swin 2E 27
Francomes SN25: Swin 2H 19
Frankel Av. SN25: Swin 5G 11
Frankland Rd. SN5: Swin 5B 26
Franklin Ho. SN3: Swin 6A 22
  (off Twickenham Cl.)
Frankton Gdns. SN3: Stra S 4A 22
Frank Warman Ct. SN3: Stra S 3A 22
Fraser Cl. SN3: Swin 1A 30
Freegrove Dr. SN15: Lyne 5D 36
FRESHBROOK 4D 26
Freshbrook Cen. SN5: Swin 5D 26
FRESHBROOK RDBT. 4D 26
Freshbrook Way SN5: Swin 4E 27
Friars Cl. SN6: Shriv 6D 16
Friday St. SN25: Swin 6F 11
Friesian Cl. SN5: Swin 1D 26
Friesland Cl. SN5: Swin 1D 26
Frilford Dr. SN3: Stra S 5H 21
Frith Copse SN5: Swin 4D 18
Fritillary Ct. SN1: Swin 3H 5
Fritillary M. SN1: Swin 3G 5
Frobisher Dr. SN3: Swin 2G 29
Frogden Rd. SN1: Swin 1C 32
Frome Rd. SN25: Swin 2A 20
Front La. SN26: Blun 1A 12

Frost Cl. SN5: Swin 2G 27
Fry Cl. SN5: Swin 4A 28
Fuller Cl. SN2: Stra S 1G 21
Fuller Gdns. SN3: S Mars 2D 22
Fullers Av. SN6: Crick 2E 7
Fullerton Wlk. SN5: Swin 4A 28
Furlong Cl. SN25: Swin 1H 19
Furze Cl. SN5: Swin 4D 18
Fyfield Av. SN2: Swin 1D 20
Fyne Cl. SN5: Swin 4E 19

G

Gable Cl. SN25: Swin 6C 12
GABLECROSS RDBT. 4D 22
Gabriel Cres. SN3: Swin 4F 11
Gainsborough Av. SN4: Woot B 2D 24
Gainsborough Ct. SN5: Swin 3D 26
Gainsborough Way SN5: Swin 3D 26
Gairlock Cl. SN5: Swin 4E 19
Gala Bingo
  Swindon 6G 21
Galen Vw. SN1: Swin 5B 28
Gallery, The SN1: Swin 5G 5
Galley Orchard SN6: Crick 2F 7
Galloway Cl. SN5: Swin 1D 26
Galloway Rd. SN5: Swin 1F 19
Galsworthy Cl. SN3: Swin 4C 30
Galton Way SN2: Swin 6H 19
Gambia St. SN1: Swin 3H 5 (2E 29)
Gamekeepers Cl. SN25: Swin 5A 12
Gantlettdene SN3: Swin 2D 30
Ganton Cl. SN3: Swin 5B 22
Ganton Way SN2: Swin 5F 21
Garden, The SN2: Stra S 1F 21
Gardens, The SN25: Swin 3B 20
Garfield Cl. SN3: Swin 1B 30
Garrard Way SN3: Swin 6G 21
Garraways SN4: Woot B 3F 25
Garrett Ho. SN3: Swin 3B 4
Garsington Dr. SN25: Swin 6F 11
Garson Rd. SN25: Swin 6C 12
Gartons Rd. SN5: Swin 1C 26
Gas La. SN6: Crick .2F 7
Gaveller Rd. SN5: Swin 5F 11
Gaynor Cl. SN25: Swin 6B 12
Gayton Way SN3: Stra S 6A 22
George Gay Gdns. SN3: Swin 4G 29
  (off Kelham Cl.)
George Selman Gdns. SN3: Swin 2H 29
  (off Twyford Cl.)
George St. SN1: Swin 4A 4 (3B 28)
George Tweed Gdns. SN5: Swin 6D 18
Gerard Wlk. SN5: Swin 2D 26
Gibbs Cl. SN3: Swin 1D 30
Gifford Rd. SN3: Stra S 3A 22
Gilberts Hill School Ho. SN1: Swin 5E 5
Gilberts La. SN6: High 2F 9
Giles Av. SN6: Crick 3E 7
Giles Rd. SN25: Swin 6G 11
Gilling Way SN3: Swin 2C 30
Gilman Cl. SN25: Swin 4B 12
Gilmore Cl. SN6: High 5F 9
  (off Brewery La.)
Giotto Cl. SN25: Swin 5E 11
Gipsy La. SN1: Swin 6E 21
Gladstone St. SN1: Swin 1F 5 (1D 28)
Gladys Plumley Gdns. SN2: Swin 6E 21
  (off Carpenters La.)
Glebe Cl. SN6: Shriv 6F 17
Glebe La. SN4: Wro 6A 32
Glebe Pl. SN6: High 4F 9
Glebe Rd. SN4: Woot B 4C 24
Gleed Cl. SN5: Pur .5A 10
Glenmore Centre, The SN5: Swin 6F 19
Glenmore Rd. SN25: Swin 1F 19
Glenville Cl. SN4: Woot B 5D 24
Glenwood Cl. SN3: Swin 6D 28
Glevum Cl. SN5: Pur 4C 10
Glevum Rd. SN3: Swin 5B 22
Globe St. SN1: Swin 6E 5 (4D 28)
Gloucester Ho. SN1: Swin 6G 21
Gloucester St. SN1: Swin 2D 4 (1C 28)
GOATACRE 6D 36
Goatacre La. SN11: Goat 6D 36
Goddard Av. SN1: Swin 1C 28
Goddard Ct. SN1: Swin 4E 29
  (off Cricklade St.)
Goddard Ho. SN1: Swin 5C 28
Godolphin Cl. SN5: Swin 6D 26
Godwin Pl. SN25: Swin 4E 29
Godwin Rd. SN3: Swin 3A 22
Goldcrest Wlk. SN3: Swin 1D 30
Goldsborough Cl. SN5: Swin 2E 27
Gold Vw. SN5: Swin 4A 28
Gooch St. SN1: Swin 1E 5 (1D 28)

Goodman La.—Hill Rd.

Goodman La. SN6: High 3E **9**
Goodrich Ct. *SN5: Swin* *4F* ***27***
(off Affleck Cl.)
Goose Ct. SN3: Swin 6F **29**
Gordon Gdns. SN1: Swin 3E **5** (2D **28**)
Gordon Rd. SN1: Swin 4F **5** (2D **28**)
Gore Cl. SN25: Swin 6A **12**
GORSE HILL 6E 21
Gosling Cl. SN4: Wan 5G **31**
Goughs Way SN4: Woot B 3E **25**
Goulding Cl. SN3: Stra S 4H **21**
Gower Cl. SN2: Stra S 4G **21**
SN5: Swin 3C **26**
Grace Wlk. SN25: Swin 6G **11**
Grafton Rd. SN2: Swin 1D **20**
Graham St. SN1: Swin 1G **5** (1E **29**)
Grailey Cl. SN3: Swin 4B **30**
Granary Cl. SN5: Swin 6C **18**
Grandison Cl. SN5: Swin 2D **26**
Grange, The SN25: Blun 4H **11**
Grange Cl. SN4: Wan 5G **31**
SN6: High 5F **9**
Grange Dr. SN3: Stra S 5H **21**
GRANGE PARK 4C 26
Grange Pk. *SN5: Swin* *3D* ***26***
(off Grange Pk. Way)
Grange Pk. Way SN5: Swin 3C **26**
Granica Cl. SN25: Swin 6G **11**
Grantham Cl. SN5: Swin 5E **27**
Grantley Cl. SN3: Swin 5H **29**
Granville St. SN1: Swin 5E **5** (2D **28**)
Grasmere SN3: Swin 5D **30**
Graythwaite Cl. SN25: Swin 6A **12**
Gt. Western Bus. Cen. SN1: Swin 3C **4** (2C **28**)
GREAT WESTERN HOSPITAL 1C 34
Gt. Western Outlet Village SN2: Swin 3A **4** (2B **28**)
Gt. Western Way SN2: Swin 1A **4** (6B **20**)
SN5: Swin 5B **26**
Green, The SN4: Lidd 3G **35**
SN4: Woot B 3F **25**
SN6: High 5E **9**
SN6: Shriv 6E **17**
SN11: Goat 6D **36**
SN15: Lyne 2E **37**
Greenaway SN4: Wan 6G **31**
Greenbridge Ind. Est. SN3: Swin 6G **21**
(not continuous)
Greenbridge Retail and Leisure Pk.
SN3: Swin 6H **21**
Greenbridge Rd. SN3: Swin 1H **29**
GREENBRIDGE RDBT. **6H 21**
Greenfields SN3: S Mars 1D **22**
Greenfields Est. SN15: Lyne 2D **36**
Greenham Wlk. *SN3: Swin* *2H* ***29***
(off Marlowe Av.)
Greenhill Rd. SN2: Swin 4H **19**
Greenlands Rd. SN2: Stra S 3F **21**
Green La. SN4: Wan 4F **31**
GREENMEADOW 2A 20
Green Mdw. Av. SN25: Swin 2A **20**
Green Rd. SN2: Stra S 3F **21**
Greensand Cl. SN25: Swin 5A **12**
Green's La. SN4: Wro 5C **32**
Green Valley Av. SN25: Swin 2A **20**
Greenway SN4: Tock 1G **37**
Greenway Cl. SN3: Swin 1A **30**
Greenway Dr. SN15: Lyne 5D **36**
Greenwich Cl. SN25: Swin 1B **20**
Greenwood Gro. SN25: Swin 6F **11**
Greenwood Pl. SN25: Swin 5G **11**
Gresham Cl. SN3: Swin 2G **29**
Grewstoke M. *SN3: Swin* *4E* ***29***
(off The Planks)
Greywethers Av. SN3: Swin 5F **29**
Griffiths Cl. SN3: Stra S 5A **22**
Grindal Dr. SN5: Swin 3C **26**
Grosmont Dr. SN5: Swin 3E **27**
Grosvenor Rd. SN1: Swin 6A **4** (4B **28**)
Groundwell Ind. Est. SN25: Swin 6E **13**
Groundwell Rd. SN1: Swin 5F **5** (3D **28**)
Grove Hill SN6: High 3E **9**
Grovelands Av. SN1: Swin 5D **28**
Grovely Cl. SN5: Swin 5D **18**
Grove Orchard SN6: High 3E **9**
Groves, The SN25: Swin 3C **20**
Groves St. SN2: Swin 2A **28**
Grundys SN3: Swin 5C **30**
Guernsey La. SN25: Swin 6G **11**
Guildford Av. SN3: Swin 5G **29**
Guild Ho. SN1: Swin 4C **4**
Guppy St. SN2: Swin 3A **4** (2A **28**)

H

Hackett Cl. SN2: Stra S 2F **21**
Hackleton Ri. SN3: Stra S 6A **22**
Hackpen Cl. SN4: Wro 3C **32**
Haddon Cl. SN5: Swin 3C **26**
Hadleigh Cl. SN5: Swin 2F **27**
Hadleigh Ri. SN3: Stra S 1H **21**
Hadrians Cl. SN3: Stra S 6B **22**
Haig Cl. SN2: Stra S 2F **21**
Hales Cl. SN15: Lyne 1C **36**
Halifax Cl. SN4: Wro 3B **32**
Hallam Moor SN3: Swin 6D **30**
Hall Cl. SN4: Wro 4B **32**
Hallsfield SN6: Crick 2D **6**
Halton Cres. SN4: Wro 6H **33**
Hamble Rd. SN25: Swin 2A **20**
Hamilton Cl. SN3: Swin 1G **29**
Hammond Cl. SN6: High 5F **9**
Hammonds SN6: Crick 2F **7**
Hampshire Cl. SN5: Swin 1D **26**
HAMPTON 5C 8
Hampton Dr. SN5: Swin 2C **26**
Ham Rd. SN4: Lidd, Wan 6H **31**
Hamstead Way SN25: Swin 5A **12**
Hamworthy Rd. SN3: Swin 2B **30**
Hanbury Rd. SN3: Swin 4G **29**
Handel St. SN2: Swin 6D **20**
HANNINGTON 3A 8
Hannington Cl. SN2: Swin 6C **12**
Hanover Ct. *SN3: Swin* *1C* ***30***
(off Kingfisher Dr.)
Hanover Ho. SN6: High 5E **9**
Hanson Cl. SN5: Swin 6E **19**
Hanwell Cl. SN25: Swin 4G **11**
Harber Ct. SN2: Swin 5D **20**
Harbour Cl. SN25: Swin 3A **20**
Harbour Mdw. SN25: Swin 2A **20**
Harcourt Rd. SN2: Swin 6B **20**
Hardie Cl. SN3: Stra S 5H **21**
Harding Ho. SN1: Swin 3C **4**
Harding St. SN1: Swin 3C **4** (2C **28**)
Hardwich Ho. *SN1: Swin* *4D* ***28***
(off Prospect Pl.)
Hardwick Cl. SN25: Swin 1B **20**
Hardy Cl. SN25: Swin 6G **11**
Harebell Cl. SN25: Swin 1G **19**
Hare Cl. SN2: Stra S 6G **13**
HARESFIELD 2F 9
Hargreaves Rd. SN25: Swin 6E **13**
Harlech Cl. SN5: Swin 4F **27**
Harlestone Rd. SN3: Stra S 6A **22**
Harold Thorpe Gdns. *SN3: Swin* *2G* ***29***
(off Middleton Cl.)
Harptree Cl. SN5: Swin 6D **18**
Harriers, The SN3: Swin 1C **30**
Harrington Wlk. SN3: Swin 1G **29**
Harris Rd. SN2: Swin 4B **20**
Harrow Cl. SN3: Stra S 5G **21**
Harrow Gro. SN15: Lyne 3F **37**
Hart Cl. SN4: Woot B 5D **24**
Hartington Rd. SN25: Swin 5F **11**
Hartland Cl. SN3: Swin 3H **29**
HARTS CLOSE 6E 37
Hartsthorn Cl. SN2: Swin 2G **19**
Harvester Cl. SN5: Swin 6C **18**
Harvey Gro. SN2: Swin 4A **20**
Hastings Ct. SN4: Wro 4B **32**
Hastings Dr. SN15: Lyne 3F **37**
Hatchers Cres. SN26: Blun 2C **12**
Hatch Rd. SN3: Stra S 2A **22**
Hatfield Cl. SN25: Swin 6H **11**
Hathaway Rd. SN2: Stra S 1F **21**
Hatherall Cl. SN3: Stra S 4B **22**
Hatherleigh Ct. SN3: Swin 2H **29**
Hatherley Rd. SN3: Swin 1A **30**
Hathersage Moor SN3: Swin 6D **30**
Hatton Gro. SN3: Swin 2G **29**
Havelock Sq. SN1: Swin 4D **4** (2C **28**)
Havelock St. SN1: Swin 4D **4** (2C **28**)
Haven Cl. SN3: Stra S 6A **22**
Havisham Dr. SN25: Swin 6F **11**
Hawfinch Cl. SN3: Swin 3D **30**
Hawker Rd. SN3: Swin 4B **30**
Hawkins St. SN2: Swin 2A **4** (1A **28**)
Hawkswood SN3: Swin 6C **22**
Hawksworth Ind. Est.
SN2: Swin 1A **4** (1B **28**)
Hawksworth Way SN2: Swin 1B **4** (1B **28**)
Hawthorn Av. SN2: Swin 4D **20**
Hayburn Rd. SN25: Swin 5H **11**
HAYDON 6H 11
Haydon Ct. SN25: Swin 1H **19**
Haydon Ct. Dr. SN25: Swin 1H **19**
Haydon End La. SN25: Swin 6F **11**
Haydonleigh Dr. SN25: Swin 1H **19**
Haydon St. SN1: Swin 2E **5** (1D **28**)
Haydon Vw. Rd. SN25: Swin 2D **20**
HAYDON WICK 2H 19
Haydon Wick Community Leisure Cen. 1H 19
Hayes Knoll SN5: Pur S 1B **10**
Hayes Knoll Station
Swindon & Cricklade Railway 2C 10
Hay La. SN4: Woot B, Wro 6B **26**
SN5: Swin 1C **26**
(not continuous)
Hay La. Caravan Pk. SN4: Wro 6D **26**
Hayle Rd. SN2: Swin 2A **28**
Hayman Cres. SN3: Swin 6F **29**
Haynes Cl. SN3: Swin 4B **30**
Haywain Cl. SN25: Swin 6D **12**
Hayward Cl. SN25: Swin 6B **12**
Hazelbury Cres. SN3: Swin 1B **30**
Hazel End SN4: Woot B 4D **24**
Hazel Gro. SN2: Swin 3D **20**
Hazells La. SN6: Shriv 6F **17**
Hazlemere Cl. SN3: Swin 4A **30**
Headlands Gro. SN2: Swin 3E **21**
Headlands Trad. Est. SN2: Swin 3F **21**
Headley Cl. SN4: Wro 6G **33**
Health Hydro, The 4C 4 (2C 28)
Heathcote Cl. SN5: Swin 6E **19**
Heath Way SN3: Stra S 6A **22**
Heaton Cl. SN25: Swin 6B **12**
Hebden Cl. SN25: Swin 5H **11**
Heberden Ho. SN6: Crick 2E **7**
Hector Rd. *SN25: Swin* *5F* ***11***
(off Hartington Rd.)
Heddington Cl. SN2: Swin 1D **20**
Hedgerow Cl. SN3: Swin 3B **30**
Hedges, The SN4: Wan 5G **31**
Hedges Cl. SN3: Stra S 3A **22**
Heights, The SN1: Swin 4B **28**
Helena Rd. SN25: Swin 4F **11**
Helmsdale SN25: Swin 2A **20**
Helmsdale Wlk. SN3: Swin 4H **29**
Helston Rd. SN3: Swin 3H **29**
Henchard Cres. SN25: Swin 1F **19**
Henley Dr. SN6: High 3F **9**
Henley Rd. SN3: Swin 4G **29**
Henman Cl. SN25: Swin 1B **20**
Henrietta Ct. *SN3: Swin* *4E* ***29***
(off Marlborough Rd.)
Henry St. SN1: Swin 3D **4** (2C **28**)
(not continuous)
Hepworth Rd. SN25: Swin 6A **12**
Herbert Harvey Ct. SN3: Stra S 6B **22**
Herbert Ludlow Gdns. SN15: Brad 2A **36**
Hereford Lawns SN3: Swin 5G **29**
Hermitage, The SN3: Swin 4E **29**
Hermitage La. SN2: Stra S 3F **21**
Heronbridge Cl. SN5: Swin 3F **27**
Heronscroft SN3: Swin 1C **30**
Herschel Cl. SN25: Swin 5E **11**
Hertford Cl. SN3: Swin 2G **29**
Hesketh Cres. SN3: Swin 5E **29**
Hewers Cl. SN4: Wan 4G **31**
Hewitt Cl. SN3: Swin 4B **30**
Hexham Cl. SN5: Swin 3E **27**
Heytsbury Gdns. SN5: Swin 4C **26**
Heywood Cl. SN2: Swin 1C **20**
Hicks Cl. SN4: Wro 4B **32**
Hidcot Ct. SN25: Swin 5H **11**
Highclere Av. SN3: Swin 4G **29**
Highdown Way SN25: Swin 4B **12**
Highfold SN4: Woot B 4E **25**
Highland Cl. SN5: Swin 1D **26**
High Mead SN4: Woot B 3E **25**
Highmoor Copse SN5: Swin 5D **18**
Highnam Cl. SN3: Stra S 5A **22**
Highridge Cl. SN5: Pur 6A **10**
High St. SN1: Swin 4E **29**
SN4: Chi 6C **34**
SN4: Wan 4H **31**
SN4: Woot B 4C **24**
SN4: Wro 5B **32**
SN5: Pur 5B **10**
SN6: Crick 3E **7**
SN6: High 5F **9**
SN6: Shriv 6E **17**
SN6: Watch 2F **17**
SN25: Swin 2H **19**
SN26: Blun 3C **12**
Highwood Cl. SN2: Swin 2G **19**
HIGHWORTH 4F 9
Highworth Golf Course 6E 9
Highworth Recreation Cen. 5E 9
Highworth Rd. SN3: S Mars 4C **14**
SN3: S Mars, Stan F 1A **22**
SN3: Stra S 3H **21**
SN6: High, Shriv 2B **16**
SN6: S Mars 4C **14**
Hillary Cl. SN25: Swin 2D **20**
Hillcrest Cl. SN1: Swin 4B **28**
Hillingdon Rd. SN3: Swin 4A **30**
HILLMEAD 6E 19
Hillmead Dr. SN5: Swin 5E **19**
Hillmead Ent. Pk. SN5: Swin 5E **19**
Hillmead Ind. Est. SN5: Swin 6E **19**
Hillocks, The SN15: Lyne 1F **37**
Hill Rd. SN6: Watch 3G **17**

44 A-Z Swindon

Hillside SN5: Pur 5C **10**
Hillside Av. SN1: Swin 6B **4** (4B **28**)
Hillside Way SN26: Blun 2B **12**
Hill Vw. SN15: Brad 2B **36**
Hill Vw. Rd. SN3: Stra S 5B **22**
Hillyard Cl. SN5: Swin 4C **26**
Hilmarton Av. SN2: Swin 1D **20**
Hilton Cl. SN1: Swin 6G **5** (3E **29**)
Hindle Way SN3: Swin 3C **30**
Hinkson Cl. SN25: Swin 4A **12**
Hinton St. SN2: Swin 6E **21**
Hobbs Row SN3: Stra S 2H **21**
(off Highworth Rd.)
Hobley Dr. SN3: Stra S 3H **21**
Hocketts Cl. SN15: Lyne 2E **37**
Hodds Hill SN5: Swin 4E **19**
HODSON 5H **33**
Hodson Rd. SN4: Chi, Hod 5A **34**
Hoggs La. SN5: Pur 5A **10**
Holbein Cl. SN5: Swin 3D **26**
Holbein Ct. SN5: Swin 3D **26**
Holbein Fld. SN5: Swin 4D **26**
Holbein Pl. SN5: Swin 3D **26**
Holbein Pl. SN5: Swin 3D **26**
Holbein Sq. SN5: Swin 4D **26**
(off Holbein Wlk.)
Holbein Wlk. SN5: Swin 4D **26**
Holbrook Way SN1: Swin 3D **4** (2C **28**)
Holburn SN5: Lyd M 1B **26**
Holdcroft Cl. SN26: Blun 2D **12**
Holden Cres. SN25: Swin 6C **12**
(off Garson Rd.)
Holinshead Pl. SN5: Swin 3D **26**
Holland Wlk. SN3: Swin 2F **29**
(off Drakes Way)
Holliday Cl. SN25: Swin 6B **12**
Hollins Moor SN3: Swin 6C **30**
Hollow Way SN15: Brad, Lyne 2A **36**
Holly Cl. SN5: Swin 4B **20**
Holmleigh SN25: Swin 2H **19**
Holmoak Ct. SN3: Swin 4E **29**
Holne Rd. SN1: Swin 1B **32**
Holst Rd. SN25: Swin 4H **11**
Home Cl. SN4: Chi 6B **34**
Home Farm SN6: High 4E **9**
(not continuous)
Home Farm La. SN6: Hann 3A **8**
Homefield SN4: Woot B 3D **24**
Home Ground SN4: Woot B 3F **25**
SN6: Crick .2D **6**
Homeleaze Rd. SN6: Shriv 3H **17**
HONDA NORTH RDBT. 1A **22**
HONDA SOUTH RDBT. 2A **22**
Honeybone Wlk. SN3: Swin 1D **30**
Honeyhill SN4: Woot B 4C **24**
Honeylight Vw. SN25: Swin 6B **12**
Honeysuckle Cl. SN25: Swin 1G **19**
Honiton Rd. SN3: Swin 3A **30**
Hook Cl. SN5: Swin 4D **18**
Hooks Hill SN5: Pur 5B **10**
Hook St. SN4: Hook, Woot B 2A **26**
SN5: Lyd T, Swin 2A **26**
Hooper Pl. SN1: Swin 4E **29**
Hopkins Orchard SN6: Crick 3E **7**
Hopton Cl. SN5: Swin 5E **27**
Horace St. SN2: Swin 2A **28**
Horcott Rd. SN5: Swin 4E **19**
Horder M. SN1: Swin 4E **29**
Hornbeam Ct. SN2: Swin 4C **20**
Hornsey Gdns. SN3: Stra S 1H **21**
HORPIT 3H **31**
Horse Fair La. SN6: Crick 2F **7**
Horsefair La. SN15: Brad 2A **36**
Horsell Cl. SN4: Woot B 3D **24**
Horseshoe Cres. SN5: Swin 5D **18**
HORSEY DOWN 2D **6**
Horsham Rd. SN3: Swin 4H **29**
Horsley Cl. SN25: Swin 4G **11**
Horton Rd. SN2: Stra S 1G **21**
Hossil La. SN6: Stan F 3A **14**
Howard Cl. SN3: Swin 2G **29**
Howse Gdn. SN2: Swin 6B **20**
Hubble Vw. SN2: Swin 5E **11**
Huddleston Cl. SN2: Swin 6E **21**
Hudson Way SN25: Swin 1B **20**
Hughes St. SN2: Swin 1H **27**
Hugo Dr. SN25: Swin 6B **12**
Hull Rd. SN2: Swin 4H **19**
Hungerford Cl. SN5: Swin 1C **26**
(off Spencer Cl.)
Hunsdon Cl. SN3: Swin 2H **29**
Hunter's Gro. SN2: Swin 5C **20**
Huntley Cl. SN3: Swin 1G **29**
Hunt's Copse Cotts. SN3: S Mars 5B **14**
(off Stirling Rd.)
Hunts Hill SN26: Blun 2C **12**
Huntsland SN4: Woot B 3E **25**
Hunts Mill Rd. SN4: Woot B 5A **24**

Hunts Ri. SN3: S Mars 6B **14**
Hunt St. SN1: Swin 6F **5** (3E **29**)
Hurst Cres. SN2: Swin 3D **20**
Hyde, The SN5: Pur 2A **18**
Hyde La. SN5: Pur 5C **10**
Hyde Rd. SN2: Stra S, Swin 6E **13**
SN4: Woot B 4E **25**
Hylder Cl. SN1: Swin 2G **19**
Hysopp Cl. SN2: Swin 2F **19**
Hythe M. SN1: Swin 4C **28**
Hythe Rd. SN1: Swin 6D **4** (3C **28**)

I

Icomb Cl. SN5: Swin 4F **27**
Idovers Dr. SN5: Swin 4F **27**
Iffley Rd. SN2: Swin 6A **20**
Iles Ct. SN11: Goat 6D **36**
Ilkeston Rd. SN25: Swin 5F **11**
Imber Wlk. SN3: Swin 6C **12**
Inglesham Rd. SN2: Swin 1D **20**
Interface Bus. Pk. SN4: Woot B 4E **25**
Inverary Rd. SN4: Wro 2B **32**
IO Centre, The SN3: Stra S 3H **21**
Ipswich St. SN2: Swin 6D **20**
Ironside Dr. SN6: Watch 3G **17**
Ironstone Cl. SN25: Swin 5H **11**
Irston Way SN5: Swin 4E **27**
Isambard Pl. SN1: Swin 2E **5**
Isambard Way SN25: Swin 5G **11**
Isis Cl. SN25: Swin 3B **20**
Isis Trad. Est. SN1: Swin 6G **21**
Island, The SN3: Swin 4D **30**
Islandsmead SN3: Swin 3B **30**
Islay Cres. SN6: High 3E **9**
Islington St. SN1: Swin 3E **5** (2D **28**)
Ivy La. SN26: Blun 2C **12**
Ixworth Cl. SN5: Swin 1D **26**

J

Jack Thorne Cl. SN5: Swin 4D **18**
Jacobs Wlk. SN3: Swin 4C **30**
Jagoda Ct. SN25: Swin 6G **11**
James Watt Cl. SN5: Swin 2B **4** (1B **28**)
James Wilkes Ho. SN25: Swin 1H **19**
Jasmine Cl. SN25: Swin 2G **19**
Jason Cl. SN25: Swin 5D **10**
Jefferies Av. SN2: Swin 4E **21**
Jenner Cl. SN4: Wan 5G **31**
Jenni Manners Ct. SN5: Swin 2G **27**
Jennings St. SN2: Swin 2A **4** (2A **28**)
Jersey Pk. SN5: Swin 5F **11**
Jewel Cl. SN5: Swin 3C **26**
Jewels Ash SN5: Pur 4C **10**
Jim Masters Ct. SN5: Swin 5D **20**
John Alder Cl. SN4: Chi 6B **34**
John Herring Cres. SN3: Stra S 5H **21**
John St. SN1: Swin 3D **4** (2C **28**)
Joiner La. SN1: Swin 4E **29**
Jole Cl. SN2: Stra S 1F **21**
Jolliffe St. SN1: Swin 5A **4** (3B **28**)
Jonson Cl. SN3: Swin 2H **29**
Jopp Cl. SN25: Swin 1F **19**
Joseph St. SN1: Swin 6B **4** (3B **28**)
Joyce Cl. SN25: Swin 5B **12**
Jubilee Est. SN5: Pur 4C **10**
Jubilee Rd. SN2: Swin 3G **19**
Juliana Cl. SN5: Swin 1D **26**
Juniper Cl. SN3: Stra S 6A **22**
Juno Way SN5: Swin 4A **28**

K

Karslake Cl. SN3: Swin 4B **30**
Keats Cl. SN4: Woot B 2E **25**
Keats Cres. SN2: Stra S 2G **21**
Keble Cl. SN3: Swin 1B **30**
Keels SN6: Crick 1D **6**
Kelham Cl. SN3: Swin 4G **29**
Kellsboro Av. SN4: Wro 3A **32**
Kelly Gdns. SN25: Swin 6A **12**
Kelmscot Rd. SN25: Swin 3D **20**
Kelvin Rd. SN3: Swin 1H **29**
Kemble Dr. SN2: Swin 1A **4** (1A **28**)
Kemerton Wlk. SN3: Swin 5H **29**
Kencot Cl. SN3: Swin 6D **12**
Kendal SN25: Swin 5A **12**
Kendrick Ind. Est. SN2: Swin 6H **19**
Kenilworth Lawns SN3: Swin 5G **29**
Kennedy Dr. SN3: Swin 4C **30**
Kennet Av. SN25: Swin 2C **20**

Kennet Rd. SN4: Wro 3B **32**
Ken Savage Cl. SN4: Wro 2H **29**
Kenton Cl. SN3: Swin 2A **30**
Kent Rd. SN1: Swin 6D **4** (3C **28**)
Kenwin Cl. SN3: Stra S 3A **22**
Kerrs Way SN4: Wro 4B **32**
Kerry Cl. SN5: Swin 1D **26**
Kershaw Rd. SN3: Swin 4B **30**
Kestrel Dr. SN3: Swin 2D **30**
Keswick Rd. SN3: Swin 5A **30**
Keycroft Copse SN5: Swin 5D **18**
Keyneston Rd. SN3: Swin 2B **30**
Keynsham Wlk. SN3: Swin 4A **30**
KEYPOINT RDBT. 4C **22**
Kibblewhite Cl. SN5: Pur 1C **26**
Kilben Cl. SN5: Swin 1C **26**
Kilda Rd. SN6: High 3D **8**
Kiln La. SN2: Swin 5A **20**
Kilsby Dr. SN3: Stra S 6A **22**
Kilsyth Cl. SN5: Swin 4D **26**
Kilve Cl. SN5: Swin 2A **30**
Kimberley Rd. SN3: Swin 4H **29**
Kimbers Fld. SN4: Wan 5G **31**
Kimbolton Cl. SN5: Swin 4D **26**
Kimmerfield Ct. SN1: Swin 3F **5**
Kimmeridge Cl. SN3: Swin 2A **30**
Kimmeridge Ct. SN1: Swin 4D **28**
(off Ripley Rd.)
King Charles Rd. SN5: Swin 4E **27**
Kingdom Cres. SN25: Swin 4G **11**
Kingfisher Dr. SN3: Swin 1C **30**
KINGFISHER RDBT. 1C **30**
King Henry Dr. SN5: Swin 4C **26**
King Ho. SN2: Swin 4B **20**
King John St. SN1: Swin 6F **5** (4E **29**)
Kings Av. SN6: High 5F **9**
Kingscote Cl. SN5: Swin 6C **18**
KINGSDOWN 1G **21**
Kingsdown Cvn. Pk. SN25: Stra S 6H **13**
Kingsdown Crematorium SN25: Stra S . . .5H **13**
Kingsdown Ind. Est. SN25: Stra S 6H **13**
Kingsdown La. SN3: Stan F 5F **13**
SN25: Blun, Stan F 4D **12**
Kingsdown Orchard SN2: Stra S 1F **21**
Kingsdown Pk. SN25: Stra S 6G **13**
Kingsdown Rd. SN2: Stra S 1G **21**
SN3: S Mars 6A **14**
SN25: Stra S 1G **21**
Kingsdown School Sports Cen. 2H **21**
KINGSHILL 6C **4** (3C **28**)
Kingshill Ct. SN1: Swin 6B **4** (4B **28**)
Kingshill Rd. SN1: Swin 6A **4** (4B **28**)
Kingsholm Ho. SN3: Swin 6A **22**
(off Twickenham Cl.)
Kingsley Av. SN4: Woot B 2D **24**
Kingsley Way SN2: Swin 1E **21**
Kingsthorpe Gro. SN3: Stra S 6B **22**
King St. SN1: Swin 3D **4** (2C **28**)
Kingsway Cl. SN3: Swin 4G **29**
Kingswood SN4: Wro 5B **32**
Kingswood Av. SN3: Swin 3H **29**
King William St. SN1: Swin 4D **28**
Kipling Gdns. SN2: Stra S 2F **21**
Kirby Cl. SN3: Swin 4G **29**
Kirkstall Cl. SN5: Swin 4F **27**
Kirktonhill Rd. SN5: Swin 2G **27**
Kishorn Cl. SN5: Swin 4E **19**
Kitchener St. SN2: Swin 5D **20**
Kitefield SN6: Crick 2E **7**
Kite Hill SN4: Wan 5G **31**
Knapp Cl. SN2: Swin 4B **20**
Knole Cl. SN25: Swin 5A **12**
Knoll, The SN1: Swin 5D **28**
Knollys Cl. SN3: Swin 2F **29**
Knolton Wlk. SN3: Swin 4H **29**
Knowlands SN6: High 3F **9**
Knowsley Rd. SN3: Swin 4H **29**
Kopernik Rd. SN25: Swin 6G **11**

L

Laburnum Dr. SN4: Woot B 2D **24**
Laburnum Rd. SN2: Swin 3D **20**
Lacock Rd. SN2: Swin 2D **20**
Lady La. SN25: Blun 4A **12**
SN25: Blun, Swin 5A **12**
SN25: Swin 6A **12**
Lady Mead SN6: Crick 2E **7**
Lagos St. SN1: Swin 2F **5** (1D **28**)
Lake Rd. SN6: Shriv 5F **17**
Lakeside SN3: Swin 5F **29**
Lake Vw. SN4: Woot B 6A **24**
Lambert Cl. SN5: Swin 5E **27**
Lambourn Av. SN3: Swin 5F **29**
Lamora Cl. SN5: Swin 6C **18**
Lampeter Rd. SN25: Swin 6F **11**
Lanac Rd. SN3: Swin 5H **21**

Lancaster Ho. SN3: Swin 3C 30
Lancaster M. SN3: S Mars 6B 14
Lancaster PI. SN3: S Mars 6B 14
Lancaster Rd. SN4: Wro 4B 32
Lancaster Sq. SN15: Lyne 3E 37
Landor Rd. SN25: Swin 4A 12
Lane, The SN2: Swin 3A 20
Langdale Dr. SN5: Swin 5E 27
Langdean Rd. SN1: Swin 1C 32
Langford Gro. SN3: Swin 4H 5 (2F 29)
Langley Rd. SN5: Swin 5E 19
Langport Cl. SN5: Swin 4E 27
Langstone Way SN5: Swin 2F 27
LANGTON PARK 6D 32
Lanhydrock Cl. SN5: Swin 4D 26
Lansbury Dr. SN2: Stra S 2G 21
Lansdowne Ho. SN3: Swin 6A 22
(off Twickenham Cl.)
Lansdown Rd. SN1: Swin 4C 28
Lapwing Cl. SN3: Swin 2D 30
SN6: Watch 2G 17
Larch Cl. SN2: Swin 4E 21
Larchmore Cl. SN25: Swin 3B 20
Larksfield SN3: Swin 1B 30
Latham Rd. SN4: Swin 4C 12
Latimer Dr. SN6: Shriv 6H 17
Latton Cl. SN2: Swin 6C 12
LATTON WHARF 1E 7
Laughton Way SN25: Swin 6B 12
Laurel Ct. SN2: Stra S 3F 21
Lavinia Wlk. SN25: Swin 6F 11
LAWN 5G 29
Lawns, The SN4: Woot B 3C 24
Lawrence Cl. SN3: Swin 4B 30
Lawton Cl. SN3: Swin 5H 29
Lea Cl. SN25: Swin 5B 12
Leamington Gro. SN3: Swin 6F 29
Leaze St. SN1: Swin 6B 28
Lechlade Rd. SN6: High 4F 9
Leicester St. SN1: Swin 4G 5 (2E 29)
Leighfield Cl. SN1: Swin 5E 5 (3D 28)
Leigh Rd. SN2: Swin 2C 20
Leighton Av. SN3: Swin 4G 29
Lennox Dr. SN3: Swin 2F 29
Lesley Ann Skeete Ct. SN3: Swin ..4A 30
Lesley Cl. SN1: Swin 6D 4 (3C 28)
Leslie Cl. SN5: Swin 4D 26
Lethbridge Rd. SN1: Swin 5D 28
Letterage Rd. SN5: Swin 4D 18
Leven SN5: Swin 5D 26
Leverton Ga. SN3: Swin 1G 33
Lewis Cl. SN25: Swin 6A 12
Lewisham Cl. SN3: Swin 3A 20
Lichen Cl. SN2: Swin 2G 19
LIDDINGTON 3G 35
Liddington St. SN2: Swin 3D 20
LIDEN 5C 30
Lidenbrook SN4: Lidd 3G 35
Liden Cen. SN3: Swin 5C 30
Liden Dr. SN3: Swin 5B 30
Lilac Ct. SN2: Swin 4C 20
Lilian Cl. SN25: Swin 6F 11
Lilian Lock Gdns. SN2: Swin 1D 20
Lillybrook SN15: Lyne 1B 36
Lilypad St. SN3: Stra S 6A 22
Lime Cl. SN15: Lyne 3G 37
Lime Kiln SN4: Woot B 2C 24
Lime Kiln Sports Cen. 2C 24
Limes Av. SN2: Swin 3C 20
Lincoln St. SN1: Swin 4F 5 (2D 28)
Linden Av. SN2: Swin 3D 20
Linden Cl. SN4: Woot B 2D 24
Linden Ct. SN1: Swin 3D 4
Linden Way SN5: Swin 4D 18
Lindisfarne SN4: Woot B 2F 25
Lineacre Cl. SN5: Swin 4C 26
Link Av. SN5: Swin 3E 27
Link Cen., The 3E 27
Linley Cl. SN1: Swin 6D 28
Linley Rd. SN26: Blun 3D 12
Linnetsdene SN3: Swin 6B 22
(not continuous)
LINSLADE RDBT. 2A 4 (2B 28)
Linslade St. SN1: Swin 3A 4 (2A 28)
Liskeard Way SN5: Swin 4E 27
Lisle Cl. SN5: Swin 3D 26
Lismore Rd. SN6: High 4D 8
Lister Rd. SN4: Wro 3C 32
Little Av. SN2: Swin 5B 20
Littlecote Cl. SN5: Swin 3G 27
LITTLECOTT 6G 37
Little London SN1: Swin 6C 5 (4E 29)
Lit. London Ct. SN1: Swin 4E 29
(off Little London)
Lit. Park Cl. SN15: Lyne 4D 36
Lockesgreen Cres. SN25: Swin 2H 19
Locks La. SN5: Pur 4B 10
Logan Cl. SN3: Swin 2F 29

Lombard Ct. SN5: Swin 4E 27
(off Westminster Rd.)
Lomond Cl. SN5: Swin 4E 19
London St. SN1: Swin 3C 4 (2C 28)
Long Acre SN5: Pur 5B 10
Longcot Cl. SN3: Stra S 5H 21
Longcot Rd. SN6: Shriv, Long 6F 17
Longfellow Cl. SN25: Swin 4B 12
Longfellow Cres. SN4: Woot B 2E 25
Longleat Gdns. SN2: Swin 2D 20
Longleaze SN4: Woot B 2D 24
Longstock Ct. SN5: Swin 2E 27
Longthorpe Cl. SN5: Swin 4G 27
Longworth Dr. SN25: Swin 5F 11
Lonsdale Cl. SN26: Blun 3D 12
Lords Cl. SN4: Wro 6H 33
Lorne St. SN1: Swin 5B 4 (3B 28)
Lotmead Bus. Pk. SN4: Wan 6E 23
Loughborough Cl. SN5: Swin 4C 26
Louviers Way SN1: Swin 6D 28
Loveage Cl. SN3: Swin 1C 30
Lovell Cl. SN3: Swin 1C 30
Loveridge Cl. SN3: Swin 6F 13
LOWER STRATTON 3H 21
LOWER VILLAGE 1C 12
LOWER WANBOROUGH 4G 31
Lowes Cl. SN5: Swin 4E 19
Loxley Wlk. SN3: Swin 5A 30
Lucerne Cl. SN4: Woot B 1C 24
SN5: Swin 6C 18
Lucetta Ri. SN25: Swin 1G 19
Luddesdown Rd. SN5: Swin 4F 27
Ludgershall Rd. SN5: Swin 4A 28
Ludlow Cl. SN3: Swin 4F 29
Lukas Cl. SN25: Swin 5A 12
Lulworth Rd. SN25: Swin 3H 19
Lumley Cl. SN5: Swin 4D 26
Luna Cl. SN25: Swin 5E 11
Lupin Cl. SN2: Stra S 3F 21
Lutyens Ga. SN3: Swin 1G 33
Lyall Cl. SN25: Blun 4A 12
Lyddon Way SN25: Swin 2A 20
Lydford Cl. SN5: Swin 6D 18
Lydiard Country Pk. 2B 26
Lydiard Country Pk. Vis. Cen. 2B 26
Lydiard Flds. SN5: Swin 5B 26
Lydiard House 2B 26
LYDIARD MILLICENT 6A 18
LYDIARD TREGOZE 2C 26
Lyme Way SN3: Swin 1B 20
Lynch Fld., The SN4: Wan 6G 31
Lyndhurst Cres. SN3: Swin 3H 29
LYNEHAM 3F 37
Lyneham Cl. SN2: Swin 6C 12
Lynmouth Rd. SN2: Swin 4A 4 (2A 28)
Lynton Rd. SN1: Swin 5H 19
Lynwood Gro. SN2: Swin 3G 19
Lypiatt Vw. SN6: Crick 3D 6
Lytchett Way SN3: Swin 2B 30

M

Mackenzie Cl. SN3: Swin 4C 30
Magdalen Rd. SN4: Wan 5G 31
Magic Rdbt., The SN1: Swin ..3H 5 (1E 29)
Magistrates' Court
Swindon 4F 5
Magnolia Ct. SN2: Swin 4C 20
Magpie La. SN3: Swin 2D 30
Maida Vale SN25: Swin 6G 11
Maiden's Cl. SN6: Watch 3G 17
Maidstone Rd. SN1: Swin 6D 4 (4C 28)
Main Dr. SN25: Blun 4A 12
Maitland Rd. SN3: Swin 1H 29
Majestic Cl. SN3: Swin 1D 26
Majors Rd. SN6: Watch 2G 17
(not continuous)
Maldwyn Cl. SN5: Swin 1C 26
Mall, The SN1: Swin 4C 28
SN6: Shriv 5G 17
Mallard Av. SN15: Lyne 4F 37
Mallard Cl. SN3: Swin 2D 30
Mallow Cl. SN2: Swin 2G 19
Malmesbury Gdns. SN3: Swin 3H 29
Malmesbury Rd. SN4: Woot B 1D 24
SN6: Crick, Leigh 5A 6
Malthouse Rd. SN3: Swin 4C 30
Maltings, The SN4: Wan 5H 31
SN4: Woot B 4C 24
Malvern Rd. SN2: Swin 4C 20
Manchester Rd. SN1: Swin 2E 5 (1D 28)
MANNINGTON 4H 27
Mannington La. SN5: Swin 3G 27
Mannington Pk. SN2: Swin 1A 28
Mannington Retail Pk. SN5: Swin ..4H 27
MANNINGTON RDBT. 3H 27

Manor Cl. SN4: Wro 5C 32
SN6: Shriv 5E 17
SN26: Blun 2D 12
Manor Cotts. SN3: S Mars 2E 23
Manor Cres. SN2: Swin 4A 20
Manor Gdns. SN2: Swin 5A 20
Manor Ho. Cl. SN4: Woot B 2C 24
Manor La. SN6: Shriv 6E 17
Manor Mdws. SN3: S Mars 2D 22
Manor Orchard SN4: Wan 5H 31
SN6: Crick 2F 7
Manor Pk. SN3: S Mars 2D 22
Manor Rd. SN1: Swin 6A 4 (3A 28)
Manor Vw. SN4: Chi 6B 34
SN4: Lidd 3G 35
Manton St. SN2: Swin 1A 4 (1A 28)
Maple SN2: Swin 4E 21
Maple Cl. SN25: Swin 3H 19
Maple Dr. SN4: Woot B 2C 24
Maple Gro. SN2: Swin 4D 20
Marbeck Cl. SN25: Swin 5H 11
March Cl. SN25: Swin 6B 12
Mardale Cl. SN5: Swin 5C 18
Margaret Leckie Ct. SN3: Swin ..2F 29
Margaret Matthews Ct. SN2: Swin ..1H 27
Marigold Cl. SN2: Swin 2G 19
Marine Cl. SN4: Wro 3C 32
Mariner Rd. SN25: Swin 5E 11
Marjoram Cl. SN2: Swin 1G 19
Markenfield SN5: Swin 4G 27
(not continuous)
Market St. SN1: Swin 4D 4 (2C 28)
Markham Cl. SN25: Swin 1G 29
Markham Pl. SN4: Wro 4A 32
Markham Rd. SN4: Wro 5B 32
Markova Cl. SN25: Swin 6F 11
Markton Cl. SN25: Swin 6F 11
Marlborough Ct. SN4: Woot B 2E 25
Marlborough La. SN1: Swin 5E 29
Marlborough Rd. SN3: Swin 5E 29
(not continuous)
SN4: Bad, Chi 4D 34
SN4: Woot B 5C 24
SN4: Wro 4C 32
Marlborough St. SN1: Swin ...5B 4 (3B 28)
Marlestones, The SN1: Swin 4C 28
Marlowe Av. SN3: Swin 1G 29
Marlowe Way SN4: Woot B 2E 25
Marney Rd. SN5: Swin 3D 26
Marsh, The SN4: Wan 6E 31
Marshall Rd. SN5: Swin 6E 19
Marsh Farm La. SN1: Swin 1F 29
Marshfield Way SN3: Stra S 4H 21
Marshgate SN1: Swin 6G 21
Marsland Rd. SN3: Swin 3E 21
Marston Av. SN2: Swin 2E 21
Marston Ga. SN3: S Mars 6B 14
Martens Cl. SN6: Shriv 6D 16
Martens Rd. SN6: Shriv 6E 17
Martinfield SN3: Swin 1C 30
Maryfield SN1: Swin 5G 5
Masefield SN4: Woot B 2E 25
Masefield Av. SN3: Swin 3F 21
Maskeleyne Way SN4: Wro 3A 32
Maslin Row SN3: Stra S 2H 21
(off Delamere Dr.)
Mason Rd. SN25: Swin 6C 12
Masons, The SN5: Pur 6A 10
Massinger Wlk. SN3: Swin 2G 29
(off Lennox Dr.)
Matley Moor SN3: Swin 6D 30
Mattocks Path SN1: Swin 1C 32
Maunsell Way SN4: Wro 3A 32
Maxey Cl. SN3: Swin 6E 19
Maxwell St. SN1: Swin 4B 4 (2B 28)
Maybold Cres. SN25: Swin 1G 19
May Cl. SN3: Swin 4D 20
May Fld. SN4: Wan 6G 31
Mayfield Cl. SN3: Swin 1A 30
Mayflower Rd. SN3: Stra S 6A 22
Mayfly Rd. SN25: Blun 5D 10
May's La. SN4: Chi 6C 34
Mazurek Way SN25: Swin 6G 11
Meadow Cl. SN4: Woot B 2D 24
Meadowcroft SN2: Stra S 2F 21
Meadow Rd. SN2: Swin 1H 27
SN6: Watch 2H 17
Meadow Springs SN5: Lyd M 3A 18
Meadowsweet Cl. SN4: Bad, Lidd ..3D 34
Meads Bus. Cen., The SN5: Swin ..2G 27
Meads Rdbt., The SN5: Swin 2G 27
Mead Way SN5: Swin 4E 19
Meares Dr. SN5: Swin 6E 19
MEDBOURNE 4F 35
Medbourne La. SN4: Bad, Lidd ...4E 35
Medgbury Pl. SN1: Swin 3G 5 (2E 29)
Medgbury Rd. SN1: Swin 3F 5 (2D 28)

Medina Way SN2: Stra S 2G 21
Medlar Ct. SN2: Swin 4C 20
Medlar Rd. SN6: Shriv 5F 17
Medway Rd. SN25: Swin 2A 20
Melbourne Cl. SN3: Swin 5G 29
Melford Wlk. SN3: Swin 1B 30
Melfort Cl. SN3: Swin 4E 19
Melksham Cl. SN2: Swin 6C 12
Mellow Ground SN25: Swin 1H 19
Melrose Cl. SN5: Swin 2F 27
Melsome Rd. SN15: Lyne 5D 36
Melstock Rd. SN25: Swin 6F 11
Melusine Rd. SN3: Stra S 6A 22
Melville Cl. SN3: Swin 2G 29
Mendip Cl. SN5: Swin 3D 20
Menham Cl. SN2: Swin 4E 21
Meriden Wlk. SN3: Swin 4A 30
MERLIN RDBT. 5C 22
Merlin Way SN3: Stra S, Swin 6C 22
(not continuous)
Merrivale Gro. SN3: Swin 4F 29
Merton Av. SN2: Stra S 2E 21
Merton St. SN1: Swin 3E 5 (2D 28)
Mervyn Webb Pl. SN2: Swin 6E 21
Metis Cl. SN25: Swin 4E 11
Mews, The SN5: Lyd M 6A 18
    SN6: High 4F 9
    SN6: Watch 3G 17
Meynell Cl. SN25: Swin 4A 12
Middle Ground SN4: Woot B 3F 25
    SN6: Crick 2D 6
MIDDLELEAZE .1C 26
Middleleaze Dr. SN5: Swin 1C 26
Middlemead La. SN6: Hann 1A 8
Middleton Cl. SN3: Swin 2G 29
Midhurst Av. SN3: Swin 3A 30
Midwinter Cl. SN5: Swin 5E 19
Midwinter Gdns. SN3: Stra S 4H 21
Milbury Wlk. SN25: Swin 1G 19
Mildenhall Way SN2: Swin 6C 12
Mildmay Cl. SN3: Swin 3C 26
Milford St. SN1: Swin 2E 5 (2D 28)
Milland Cl. SN25: Swin 6C 12
(off Garson Rd.)
Millbuck Cl. SN2: Swin 5F 21
Mill Cl. SN4: Chi 6C 34
    SN4: Wro 4C 32
Mill Ct. SN3: Swin 5E 29
Miller Cl. SN5: Swin 6C 18
Millgrove St. SN25: Swin 5G 11
Mill La. SN1: Swin 5A 28
    SN4: Wro 6H 27
    SN6: Stan F 2H 13
Millstone Cl. SN4: Woot B 4E 25
Milne Way SN3: Stra S 1A 22
Milston Av. SN2: Swin 1D 20
Milton Rd. SN1: Swin 4C 4 (2C 28)
Milton's Way SN4: Woot B 4B 24
Milverton Ct. SN3: Swin 3H 29
(off Banwell Av.)
Minety Rd. SN2: Swin 1C 20
Minnow Cl. SN25: Blun 5D 10
Minster Cl. SN5: Swin 5A 12
Mint Cl. SN2: Swin 2G 19
Mir Cres. SN25: Swin 5E 11
Mistletowe Ct. SN1: Swin 5B 28
(off Pasteur Dr.)
Mitchell Cl. SN4: Woot B 3C 24
Moat Wlk. SN4: Wro 5C 32
Monet Cl. SN25: Swin 6A 12
Monkton Cl. SN3: Swin 4A 30
Monmouth Cl. SN3: Swin 4G 29
Montagu St. SN1: Swin 1A 28
Monteagle Cl. SN5: Swin 4D 26
Montgomery Av. SN2: Swin 4E 19
Montrose Cl. SN2: Swin 4H 19
MOONRAKERS RDBT. 3E 21
Moore Cl. SN4: Wro 2D 32
Moorhen Cl. SN3: Swin 3D 30
Moorings, The SN1: Swin 6A 4 (3B 28)
Moormead Rd. SN4: Wro 4C 32
Moors, The SN5: Lyd M 6A 18
Moray Rd. SN3: Swin 5F 21
MOREDON 3H 19
Moredon Golf Course 4H 19
Moredon Pk. SN2: Swin 3G 19
Moredon Rd. SN2: Swin 3H 19
Moresby Cl. SN5: Swin 2F 27
Morie Cl. SN5: Swin 5E 19
Morley St. SN1: Swin 5E 5 (2D 28)
Morrison St. SN2: Swin 1A 28
Morris St. SN2: Swin 2A 4 (1H 27)
(not continuous)
Morse Gdns. SN5: Swin 2F 27
Morse St. SN1: Swin 5D 4 (3C 28)
Morstone Rd. SN4: Woot B 4C 24
Mortimer Cl. SN5: Swin 1E 27
Mortree Ct. SN6: Shriv 6E 17

Mountbatten Ho. SN2: Swin 4B 20
(off Tovey Rd.)
Mountings, The SN4: Wro 2C 32
Muirfield SN25: Swin 5G 11
Mulberry SN2: Swin 4F 21
Mulberry Gro. SN2: Swin 4B 20
Mulberrys, The SN4: Woot B 3C 24
Mulcaster Av. SN5: Swin 3C 26
Mundy Av. SN3: Swin 4B 30
Munro Cl. SN3: Swin 2F 29
Murdock Rd. SN3: Swin 2D 30
Murrayfield Ho. SN3: Swin 6A 22
(off Twickenham Cl.)
Muscovey Cl. SN15: Lyne 3E 37
Mustang Way SN3: Swin 3F 19
Mycroft Rd. SN25: Swin 6G 11
Myrtle Gdns. SN2: Swin 4D 20

N

Nantwich SN5: Swin 5D 26
Napier Cl. SN2: Swin 1A 4 (1B 28)
Nash Cl. SN25: Swin 4B 12
National Monuments Record Cen. . . .2B 4 (1B 28)
Naunton Rd. SN3: Swin 2H 29
Neighbourhood Cen. SN25: Swin 4B 12
Nell Hill SN6: Hann 3A 8
Nelson St. SN1: Swin 5A 4 (3A 28)
Neptune Cres. SN3: Stra S 6A 22
Ness Cl. SN5: Swin 4E 19
Netherton Cl. SN3: Swin 4A 30
Nevis Cl. SN5: Swin 4E 19
Newark Cl. SN5: Swin 5E 27
Newbridge Cl. SN1: Swin 2E 5
New Bridge Sq. SN1: Swin 2E 5 (2D 28)
Newburgh Ho. SN6: High 4E 9
Newburgh Pl. SN6: High 4E 9
Newburn Cres. SN1: Swin 5A 4 (3A 28)
Newbury Dr. SN5: Swin 5E 27
Newcastle St. SN1: Swin 4G 5 (2E 29)
New College Dr. SN3: Swin 3G 29
New College Wlk. SN3: Swin 3G 29
(off Bilborough Dr.)
Newcombe Dr. SN2: Swin 1A 4 (6B 20)
Newhall St. SN1: Swin 5D 4 (3C 28)
Newland Rd. SN25: Swin 3B 20
Newmeadow Copse SN5: Swin 5D 18
Newport St. SN1: Swin 4E 29
New Rd. SN4: Chi 6C 34
    SN4: Woot B .4C 24
    SN5: Wid 4C 10
Newson Rd. SN25: Swin 1G 19
Newstead Cl. SN5: Swin 6A 12
Newth's La. SN5: Pur S 2A 10
Newton Way SN2: Swin 2D 20
NEW ZEALAND .5B 36
NHS WALK-IN CENTRE (SWINDON) 3E 5
NHS WALK-IN CENTRE (SWINDON, CLOVER CENTRE)
. . . . .1D 34
Nicholas Ct. SN1: Swin 5D 28
Nightingale La. SN3: S Mars 2E 23
Nightwood Copse SN5: Swin 5D 18
Nindum Rd. SN3: Stra S 5A 22
NINE ELMS 6C 18
Nocton Rd. SN4: Wro 6H 33
Nolan Cl. SN25: Swin 4A 12
Norbury Ct. SN5: Pur 5C 10
Norcliffe Rd. SN3: Swin 4A 30
Noredown Way SN4: Woot B 4D 24
Nore Marsh Rd. SN4: Woot B 4D 24
Norfolk Cl. SN3: Swin 2G 29
Normandy Rd. SN4: Wro 6H 33
Norman Rd. SN2: Swin 6D 20
Norris Cl. SN4: Chi 6B 34
Northampton St. SN1: Swin 4G 5 (2E 29)
North Bank Ri. SN4: Woot B 3E 25
Northbourne Rd. SN25: Swin 5B 12
Northbrook Rd. SN2: Swin 5C 20
North Dr. SN25: Blun 4A 12
Northern Rd. SN2: Swin 4B 20
Northfield Way SN3: Swin 1A 30
NORTHFORD 4G 17
Northford Cl. SN6: Shriv 4F 17
Northford Hill SN6: Watch 4G 17
Northford Ind. Est. SN6: Shriv 4F 17
North Leaze Cl. SN2: Swin 3A 20
North Mdw. Rd. SN6: Crick 2D 6
North Star Av. SN2: Swin 1C 4 (6C 20)
North Star Ho. SN2: Swin 2C 4 (1C 28)
NORTH STAR RDBT. 6C 20
North St. SN1: Swin 6E 5 (3D 28)
    SN6: Watch 3G 17
North Vw. SN6: High 4E 9
North Vw. Ho. SN5: Pur 6B 10
North Wall SN6: Crick 2E 7
NORTH WROUGHTON 3C 32
Norton Gro. SN3: Swin 5H 5 (3E 29)

Norwood Cl. SN3: Swin 4C 30
Noyes Cl. SN25: Swin 1F 19
Nuffield Cl. SN5: Swin 6E 19
Nuffield Health
    Swindon 6G 21
Nunwick Way SN1: Swin 6B 28
Nurseries, The SN1: Swin 6C 4 (4C 28)
Nursery Cl. SN4: Wro 5B 32
Nuthatch Cl. SN3: Swin 2D 30
Nutmeg Cl. SN25: Swin 2G 19
Nyland Rd. SN3: Swin 1B 30
NYTHE 1B 30
Nythe Rd. SN3: Stra S 5A 22

O

Oakapple Cl. SN4: Wan 5H 31
Oak Dr. SN6: High .5E 9
Oakford Wlk. SN3: Swin 2H 29
Oak Gdn. SN3: Stra S 2H 21
Oakham Cl. SN5: Swin 4F 27
Oakhurst Way SN2: Swin 5E 11
Oakie Cl. SN25: Swin 4A 12
Oak Rd. SN6: Watch 3F 17
Oaks, The SN4: Woot B 3E 25
Oaksey Rd. SN2: Swin 2D 20
Oak Tree Av. SN2: Swin 3E 21
Oakwood Rd. SN5: Swin 1F 27
Oasis Leisure Cen., The 1C 4 (1C 28)
OASIS RDBT. 1C 4 (6C 20)
Oasthouse Cl. SN5: Swin 6D 18
Oberek Cl. SN3: Swin 6G 11
Oberon Way SN25: Swin 1B 20
Ockwells SN6: Crick 3E 7
(off The Forty)
OCOTAL RDBT. 1H 5 (1E 29)
Ocotal Way SN1: Swin 1H 5 (6E 21)
Odstock Rd. SN2: Swin 6D 12
Offerton Rd. SN1: Swin 6B 28
Okebourne Pk. SN3: Swin 5B 30
Okeford Cl. SN3: Swin 1B 30
OKUS 5B 28
Okus Gro. SN2: Stra S 2E 21
Okus Rd. SN1: Swin 4A 28
Old Bakery, The SN2: Swin 6A 20
    SN5: Lyd M 6A 18
(off the Street)
Old Brickyard, The SN2: Swin 5A 20
Old Ct. SN4: Woot B 4C 24
Old Dairy Cl. SN2: Stra S 3F 21
Oldenburg Cl. SN5: Swin 4E 19
Old Joinery, The SN1: Swin 5E 5
Old Lady La. SN26: Blun 3C 12
Oldlands Wlk. SN3: Swin 5A 30
Old Malmesbury Gdns. SN4: Woot B 1D 24
Old Malmesbury Rd. SN4: Woot B 1D 24
Old Mill La. SN3: Swin 5E 29
Old School, The SN1: Swin 4F 5
Old School Ct. SN3: Swin 2A 30
OLD SHAW 1D 26
Old Shaw La. SN5: Swin 6D 18
(not continuous)
Old Surgery Cl. SN5: Pur 5C 10
OLD TOWN 6G 5 (4E 29)
Old Vicarage La. SN3: S Mars 2D 22
Olive Gro. SN25: Swin 3C 20
Oliver Cl. SN5: Swin 2C 26
Olivier Rd. SN25: Swin 6C 12
Omdurman St. SN2: Swin 5C 20
Open Cl. SN3: Swin 6F 29
Oppenheimer Cen. SN3: Swin 1H 29
Orange Cl. SN6: High 4F 9
Orbital Shop. Pk. SN25: Swin 6H 11
Orbit Cen., The SN5: Swin 2H 27
Orchard, The SN3: Swin 1G 33
    SN4: Chi 6D 34
    SN5: Lyd M 6A 18
Orchard Cl. SN4: Wan 5G 31
Orchard Gdns. SN5: Pur 6A 10
Orchard Gro. SN2: Stra S 3E 21
Orchard Ind. Est. SN2: Swin 5A 20
Orchard La. SN4: Tock 2H 37
Orchard Mead SN4: Woot B 3F 25
Orchard Pk. SN4: Woot B 4B 24
Orchid Cl. SN25: Swin 3D 20
Orchid Ct. SN25: Swin 6G 11
Orkney Cl. SN5: Swin 1E 27
Orlando Cl. SN5: Swin 3C 26
Orrin Cl. SN5: Swin 4E 19
Orwell Cl. SN25: Swin 1B 20
Osborne St. SN2: Swin 6C 20
Osprey Cl. SN3: Swin 2D 30
Osterley Rd. SN25: Swin 6H 11
Otter Row SN3: Swin 6A 22
Otter Way SN4: Woot B 3E 25
Overbrook SN3: Swin 4A 30
Overton Gdns. SN3: Stra S 4A 22

OVERTOWN 6E 33
Overtown Hill SN4: Wro 5D 32
Owen Ct. SN3: Stra S 5H 21
Owl Cl. SN3: Swin 2D 30
Owlets, The SN3: Swin 2D 30
Oxford Gdns. SN1: Swin 4C 28
Oxford Rd.
   SN3: S Mars, Stra S 5H 21
Oxford Sq. SN6: Watch 3F 17
Oxford St. SN1: Swin 3C 4 (2C 28)

P

Pack Hill SN4: Wan 6E 31
Packington Cl. SN5: Swin 1E 27
Paddington Dr. SN5: Swin 2H 27
Paddock, The SN6: High 5F 9
Paddock Cl. SN25: Swin 1A 20
Paddocks, The SN3: Stra S 4H 21
Padstow Rd. SN2: Swin 3A 28
Pakenham Rd. SN3: Swin 4A 30
Palmers Way SN4: Wan 5G 31
Palomino Pl. SN5: Swin 5A 10
Parade, The SN1: Swin 3D 4 (2C 28)
   SN5: Pur 6A 10
Paradise Path SN6: High 4F 9
Paramount SN1: Swin 4F 5
Parhams Ct. SN4: Woot B 3D 24
Parham Wlk. SN5: Swin 3C 26
Park & Ride 1D 32
Park Av. SN6: High 5F 9
   SN6: Shriv .6G 17
Park Farm SN25: Swin 3H 19
Park Gdns. SN6: Crick 2D 6
Parklands Rd. SN3: Swin 6H 5 (3F 29)
Park La. SN1: Swin 4A 4 (2B 28)
   SN5: Lyd M 6A 18
PARK NORTH .3H 29
Parkside SN3: Stra S 3H 21
   SN5: Pur 2A 18
PARK SOUTH .4H 29
Park Springs SN5: Swin 3F 27
Parkstone Wlk. SN3: Swin 5A 30
   (off Cranmore Av.)
Park St. SN3: Stra S 4B 22
Park Vw. SN2: Stra S 2F 21
Park Vw. Dr. SN5: Lyd M 6A 18
Parr Cl. SN5: Swin 2D 26
Parsley Cl. SN2: Swin 1G 19
Parsloes Cl. SN4: Wro 6H 33
Parsonage Ct. SN6: High 4F 9
Parsonage Farm Cl. SN6: Crick 3E 7
Parsonage Rd. SN3: Stra S 3H 21
Parson's La. SN6: Hann 3A 8
Parson's Way SN4: Woot B 4D 24
Partridge Cl. SN3: Swin 2D 30
Passmore Cl. SN3: Swin 1D 30
Pasteur Dr. SN1: Swin 5B 28
Pasture Cl. SN3: Swin 1H 27
Pathfinder Way SN25: Swin 5E 11
Patney Wlk. SN3: Swin 6C 12
Paulet Cl. SN5: Swin 4D 26
Pauls Cft. SN6: Crick 3F 7
Paven Cl. SN5: Pur 5A 10
Pavenhill SN5: Pur 5A 10
Pavenhill Courtyard SN5: Pur 5A 10
Pavilion Cl. SN1: Swin 2H 5 (1F 29)
Paxton Cl. SN1: Swin 4D 28
   (off Prospect Pl.)
Peak, The SN5: Pur 6B 10
Peaks Down SN5: Swin 4E 19
Pearce Cl. SN2: Swin 6F 13
Pearl Rd. SN5: Swin 1C 26
Pear Tree Cl. SN5: Pur 4C 10
PEATMOOR 5D 18
Peatmoor Village Cen. SN5: Swin 5D 18
   (off Shearwood Rd.)
Peatmoor Way SN5: Swin 5D 18
Peglars SN1: Swin 6H 27
Peglars Way SN1: Swin 5A 28
Pembroke Cen. SN2: Swin 5H 19
Pembroke Gdns. SN25: Swin 3H 19
Pembroke St. SN1: Swin 6E 5 (4D 28)
Pencarrow Cl. SN25: Swin 6H 11
Pen Cl. SN3: Swin 2B 20
Pendennis Rd. SN5: Swin 5D 26
Penfold Gdns. SN1: Swin 4D 28
PENHILL 1D 20
Penhill Dr. SN2: Swin 1C 20
Pennine Way SN25: Swin 5A 12
Pennycress Cl. SN3: Swin 2H 19
Pennyhooks La. SN6: Shriv 3D 16
Penny La. SN3: Swin 1G 29
Penrose Wlk. SN3: Swin 4D 26
   (off Dulverton Av.)
Pentridge Cl. SN3: Swin 1B 30
Pentylands Cl. SN6: High 3E 9

Penzance Dr. SN2: Swin 4A 4 (3H 27)
   SN5: Swin .3H 27
Pepperbox Hill SN5: Swin 4E 19
Percheron Cl. SN5: Swin 1D 26
Percy St. SN2: Swin 2A 4 (1A 28)
   (not continuous)
Peregrine Cl. SN3: Swin 6C 22
Periwinkle Cl. SN2: Swin 3F 19
Perry's La. SN4: Wro 4B 32
Peter Furkins Ct. SN1: Swin 5A 4
Petersfield Rd. SN3: Swin 4A 30
Petter Cl. SN4: Wro 3C 32
PEVENSEY RDBT. 4F 27
Pevensey Way SN5: Swin 3F 27
Pewsham Rd. SN2: Swin 1E 21
Pheasant Cl. SN3: Swin 2D 30
Phillips La. SN1: Swin 4E 29
Phoebe Way SN25: Swin 5E 11
Phoenix Gdns. SN25: Swin 5E 11
PICCADILLY RDBT. 1B 30
Pickford Way SN25: Swin 6B 12
Pickwick Cl. SN2: Stra S 1F 21
Picton Rd. SN5: Swin 1D 26
Piernik Cl. SN5: Swin 6H 11
Pigeon Ho. La. SN3: Stra S 3H 21
Pike Ho. Cl. SN6: Crick 2D 6
Pilgrim Cl. SN3: Swin 1D 26
Pilgrims Cl. SN6: Watch 5H 17
Pilton Cl. SN5: Swin 6C 18
Pine Cl. SN2: Swin 4F 21
PINEHURST 3D 20
Pinehurst Rd. SN2: Swin 3D 20
Pinehurst Rd. SN2: Swin 5C 20
   (not continuous)
Pinetree Ri. SN25: Swin 3C 20
Pinnacle, The SN1: Swin 4E 29
Pinnegar Way SN3: Swin 2D 30
Pinnock's Pl. SN2: Stra S 2G 21
Pintail Cl. SN15: Lyne 4F 37
Pinto Cl. SN5: Swin 3F 19
Pioneer Cl. SN5: Swin 1D 26
Pioneer Rd. SN25: Swin 5E 11
Pipers Cl. SN4: Woot B 5C 24
PIPERS RDBT. .6E 29
Pipers Way SN3: Swin 1D 32
Pipitdene SN3: Swin 1C 30
Pitchens, The SN4: Wro 5C 32
   (not continuous)
Pitt Cl. SN1: Swin 1F 29
Pittsfield SN6: Crick 3E 7
Planks, The SN3: Swin 4E 29
Plattes Cl. SN3: Swin 6E 19
Play Cl. SN5: Pur 5C 10
Plaza, The SN1: Swin 4E 5
Pleydell Rd. SN1: Swin 6D 28
Pleydells SN6: Crick 2E 7
Plummer Cl. SN4: Wro 4B 32
Plymouth St. SN1: Swin 3G 5 (2E 29)
Poachers Way SN25: Swin 5A 12
Polaris Ho. SN2: Swin 1D 4 (1C 28)
Polaris Way SN2: Swin 1D 4 (1C 28)
Polonez Ct. SN25: Swin 6G 11
Poltondale SN3: Swin 1C 30
Pond St. SN25: Swin 2D 12
Pontings Cl. SN26: Blun 1A 20
Ponting St. SN1: Swin 1F 5 (1D 28)
Poole Rd. SN5: Swin 3H 19
Poor St. SN5: Pur 6A 10
Pope Cl. SN25: Swin 1A 20
Poplar Av. SN2: Swin 4D 20
Popplechurch Dr. SN3: Swin 1D 30
Portal Pl. SN15: Lyne 4E 37
Portal Rd. SN2: Swin 4D 20
Porth Cl. SN25: Swin 5F 11
Portland Av. SN1: Swin 4C 20
Portmore Cl. SN5: Swin 4F 19
Portsmouth St. SN1: Swin 3G 5 (2E 29)
Portwell SN6: Crick 3E 7
Poseidon Cl. SN25: Swin 6E 11
Postmill Dr. SN4: Woot B 4E 25
Potterdown Rd. SN2: Swin 1D 20
Poulton St. SN2: Swin 6D 20
Pound Cl. SN15: Lyne 2E 37
Pound La. SN6: Swin 4C 20
Pound Rd. SN6: High 3E 9
Powdrill's Yd. SN3: Stra S 4G 21
Powell Pl. SN4: Swin 4H 19
Poynings Way SN5: Swin 4E 19
Premier Ho. SN1: Swin 2E 5 (1D 28)
PRESTON 3F 37
Preston La. SN15: Lyne, Pres 3F 37
Priam Ho. SN1: Swin 3B 4
Primrose Cl. SN25: Swin 1G 19
Primrose Hill SN4: Tock 1H 37
Princess Gdns. SN4: Woot B 3D 24
Princes St. SN1: Swin 3F 5 (2D 28)
PRINNELS, THE 2C 26

Prior's Hill SN4: Wro 5C 32
Priory, The SN6: Crick 1F 7
Priory Grn. SN6: High 4F 9
   (not continuous)
Priory Mnr. SN25: Swin 5H 11
Priory Rd. SN3: Swin 4H 29
Pritchard Cl. SN2: Swin 1G 21
Prospect Hill SN1: Swin 6F 5 (3D 28)
PROSPECT HOSPICE 4D 32
Prospect Pl. SN1: Swin 6F 5 (4D 28)
Prospero Way SN25: Swin 6F 11
Proud Cl. SN5: Pur 6B 10
PRY, THE 1C 18
Pulsar Rd. SN25: Swin 5E 11
Purbeck Cl. SN3: Swin 1B 30
Purcell Rd. SN25: Swin 4G 11
Purley Av. SN3: Swin 5A 30
Purley Cl. SN4: Wro 4C 32
Purley Rd. SN4: Lidd 1E 35
Purslane Cl. SN2: Swin 3F 19
PURTON 5C 10
Purton Ct. SN5: Pur 5C 10
Purton Mus. 5C 10
Purton Rd. SN5: Swin 4D 18
   (not continuous)
PURTON STOKE 2A 10

Q

Quadrillion Ind. Est. SN5: Swin 1G 27
Quakers La. SN5: Goat 6C 36
Quakers Wlk. SN11: Goat 6D 36
Quarries, The SN1: Swin 5D 28
Quarrybrook Cl. SN3: S Mars 1D 22
Quarry Cres. SN6: High 4E 9
Quarry M. SN1: Swin 5D 28
Quarry Rd. SN1: Swin 4D 28
Queenborough SN5: Swin 4F 27
Queen Elizabeth Dr. SN25: Swin 6F 11
Queens Av. SN6: High 3F 9
Queens Dr. SN3: Swin 3H 5 (2F 29)
   (not continuous)
QUEENSFIELD .1E 21
Queensfield SN3: Stra S 1E 21
Queens Rd. SN4: Woot B 3D 24
   SN6: Hann, High 3A 8
Queen St. SN1: Swin 3D 4 (2C 28)
Queitin Rd. SN3: Swin 5E 29

R

Radcot Cl. SN5: Swin 5D 18
Radley Cl. SN3: Swin 1B 30
Radnor St. SN1: Swin 6B 4 (3B 28)
Radstock Av. SN3: Swin 2A 30
Radway Rd. SN3: Stra S 3G 21
RAF Lyneham (Disused) 3A 36
Raggett St. SN1: Swin 6E 5 (3D 28)
Raglan Cl. SN3: Swin 6F 29
Rainer Cl. SN3: Stra S 3A 22
Rainham Rd. SN25: Swin 5A 12
Raleigh Av. SN3: Swin 2G 29
RAMLEAZE 2D 26
Ramleaze Dr. SN5: Swin 1D 26
Ramsbury Av. SN2: Swin 1C 20
Ramsden Rd. SN5: Swin 5C 26
RAMSDEN RDBT. 5C 26
Ramsthorn Cl. SN25: Swin 2G 19
Randall Cres. SN5: Swin 6D 18
Randolph Cl. SN3: Swin 3G 29
Rannoch Cl. SN5: Swin 4E 19
Ransome Cl. SN5: Swin 6E 19
Ratcoombe Rd. SN5: Swin 4D 18
Ravenglass Rd. SN5: Swin 2F 27
Ravenscroft SN3: Swin 6B 22
Ravensdale SN1: Swin 6B 28
Ravenseft Pk. SN3: Swin 5H 19
Ravens Wlk. SN4: Woot B 3F 25
Rawlings Cl. SN3: S Mars 2D 22
Rawston Cl. SN3: Swin 2B 30
Ray Cl. SN25: Swin 2B 20
Raybrook Cres. SN2: Swin 6C 20
Rayfield Gro. SN2: Swin 6C 20
Reading St. SN1: Swin 3C 4 (2C 28)
Read St. SN1: Swin 5B 4 (3B 28)
Recreation Rd. SN6: Shriv 5E 17
Rectory Cl. SN4: Wro 6H 33
Rectory La. SN6: Crick 2F 7
Redbridge Cl. SN5: Swin 4A 28
Redcap Gdns. SN5: Swin 1D 26
Redcliffe St. SN2: Swin 3A 4 (2A 28)
Redcross Pl. SN1: Swin 6B 4 (3B 28)
Reddings Ho. SN3: Swin 6A 22
   (off Twickenham Cl.)
Red Gables Cl. SN5: Pur 6A 10
Redhouse Gdns. SN25: Swin 5G 11

Redhouse Way—Shrewsbury Rd.

Redhouse Way SN25: Swin 5F 11
REDLANDS 1E 15
Redlands Cl. SN6: High 6F 9
Red Lion La. SN6: Crick 2F 7
Red Lion M. *SN6: High* *4F 9*
(off Sheep St.)
Red Lodge Cl. SN4: Woot B 5D 24
Redlynch Cl. SN2: Swin 1D 20
Redposts Dr. SN5: Swin 4H 27
Redruth Cl. SN3: Swin 3A 30
Reed Ct. SN3: Stra S 5B 22
Reeds SN6: Crick 2D 6
Reema Houses SN6: Seven 3G 15
Reeves Cl. SN3: Swin 4B 30
Regent Cir. SN1: Swin 5E 5 (3D 28)
Regent Cl. SN1: Swin 4E 5 (2D 28)
Regent Pl. SN1: Swin 4E 5 (2D 28)
Regents Pl. SN1: Swin 6G 21
Regent St. SN1: Swin 4D 4 (2C 28)
Reid's Piece SN5: Pur 6B 10
Renoir Cl. SN25: Swin 4B 12
RESTROP 6A 10
Restrop Rd. SN5: Pur, Rest 6A 10
Restrop Vw. SN5: Pur 5A 10
Retingham Way SN3: Stra S 1H 21
Retreat, The SN6: High 4E 9
Revell Cl. SN2: Stra S 2F 21
Reynolds Way SN25: Swin 4B 12
Rhine Cl. SN5: Swin 4A 28
Rhuddlan SN5: Swin 4E 27
Richard Jefferies Gdns. SN4: Chi 6C 34
Richard Jefferies Mus. 6A 30
Richards Cl. SN4: Woot B 4C 24
Richmond Ho. SN3: Swin 3C 30
(Edison Pk.)
SN3: Swin 6A 22
(off Twickenham Cl.)
Richmond Rd. SN2: Swin 5B 20
Ridge, The SN26: Blun 2C 12
Ridge Grn. SN5: Swin 1E 27
Ridge Nether Moor SN3: Swin 6D 30
Ridgeway, The SN4: Bad, Chi 6D 34
RIDGEWAY BMI HOSPITAL 4C 32
Ridgeway Cl. SN2: Swin 4A 20
Ridgeway Leisure Centre 3C 32
Ridgeway Rd. SN2: Stra S 1F 21
Ridings, The SN2: Swin 6B 20
Rigel Cl. SN25: Swin 5E 11
Ringsbury Cl. SN5: Pur 6A 10
Ringwood Cl. SN3: Swin 2A 30
Rinsdale Cl. SN5: Swin 5E 19
Ripley Rd. SN1: Swin 4D 28
Ripon Way SN3: Swin 5H 29
Ripple Fld. SN5: Swin 4E 27
Risingham Mead SN5: Swin 3F 27
Rivenhall Rd. SN5: Swin 3F 27
Riverdale Cl. SN1: Swin 6D 28
Riverdale Wlk. SN1: Swin 6D 28
Rivergate SN5: Swin 6F 19
RIVERMEAD 6F 19
Rivermead Dr. SN5: Swin 6F 19
Rivermead Ind. Est. SN5: Swin 6F 19
River Ray Est. SN2: Swin 1G 27
Rivers Way SN6: High 4E 9
RMCS Shrivenham Golf Club 5G 17
Roberts Cl. SN4: Wro 5C 32
Robins Cl. SN4: Woot B 3F 25
Robinsgreen SN3: Swin 1C 30
Robinson Cl. SN3: Swin 2C 30
Roche Cl. SN3: Swin 4C 30
Rochester Cl. SN5: Swin 4E 27
Rochford Cl. SN5: Swin 3D 26
Rockdown Ct. SN2: Swin 2E 21
RODBOURNE 5A 20
RODBOURNE CHENEY 3B 20
Rodbourne Rd. SN2: Swin 1A 4 (6A 20)
(not continuous)
RODBOURNE RDBT. 6A 20
Rodway SN4: Wan 5G 31
Rodwell Cl. SN3: Swin 4H 29
Roebuck Cl. SN4: Woot B 3E 25
Rogers Cl. SN3: Swin 1H 29
Rokeby Ho. SN2: Swin 3B 4
Rolleston St. SN1: Swin 5F 5 (3D 28)
Roman Cres. SN1: Swin 5C 28
Roman Wlk. SN6: Watch 2H 17
Roman Way SN6: High 5E 9
Romney Way SN5: Swin 2D 26
Romsey St. SN2: Swin 1A 28
Rope Yd. SN4: Woot B 4C 24
Rope Yd. Ct. SN4: Woot B 4C 24
Rosary, The SN4: Woot B 3D 24
Rosebery St. SN1: Swin 1G 5 (1E 29)
Rose Ct. SN4: Woot B 3D 24
Rosedale Rd. SN3: Swin 4A 30
Rosehill Cl. SN15: Brad 1B 36
Rosemary Cl. SN2: Swin 1G 19
Rose St. SN2: Swin 1A 28
Rosetta Cl. SN25: Swin 5E 11
Rose Wlk. SN25: Swin 1A 20
Rosewood Ct. *SN3: Swin* *5C 30*
(off Liden Dr.)
Ross Gdns. SN3: Stra S 2H 21
Rother Cl. SN25: Swin 1A 20
Rotten Row SN4: Wan 5G 31
ROUGHMOOR 4D 18
Roughmoor Farm Cl. SN5: Swin 5D 18
Roughmoor Way SN5: Swin 1D 26
Roundhills Mead SN6: High 2F 9
Round Ho. Dr. SN4: Woot B 4E 25
Roundway Down SN5: Swin 5E 27
Roves Farm Vis. Cen. 6G 15
Roves La. SN6: Seven 3G 15
Row, The SN2: Swin 5E 21
Rowan SN2: Swin 4F 21
Rowan Ct. SN1: Swin 5B 28
Rowan Dr. SN4: Woot B 4D 24
Rowan Ho. SN1: Swin 3D 4
Rowan Rd. SN2: Swin 3B 20
Rowborough La. SN3: S Mars 3E 23
Rowland Hill Cl. SN3: Swin 4D 30
Rowton Heath Way SN5: Swin 4D 26
ROYAL WOOTON BASSETT 3C 24
Royston Rd. SN3: Swin 4H 29
Rubens Cl. SN25: Swin 4A 12
Ruckley Gdns. SN3: Stra S 4A 22
Rushall Cl. SN2: Swin 1C 20
Rushmere Path SN25: Swin 1A 20
Rushton Rd. SN3: Swin 5H 29
Ruskin Av. SN2: Stra S 3G 21
Ruskin Dr. SN4: Woot B 2E 25
Russell Wlk. SN3: Swin 2F 29
Russley Cl. SN5: Swin 5C 18
Rutland Rd. SN3: Swin 3G 29
Ruxley Cl. SN4: Woot B 4C 24
Ryan Cl. SN5: Swin 4E 19
Rycote Cl. SN5: Swin 2D 26
Rydal Cl. SN25: Swin 1A 20
Rye Cl. SN5: Swin 1D 26
Rylands Way SN4: Woot B 3D 24
Rylane SN1: Swin 6C 28
Rysy Ct. SN25: Swin 6H 11

S

Sackville Cl. SN3: Swin 1G 29
Saddleback Rd. SN5: Swin 1D 26
Sadler Wlk. SN3: Swin 3G 29
Saffron Cl. SN4: Woot B 1D 24
SN25: Swin 3H 19
Sage Cl. SN2: Swin 1G 19
St Albans Cl. SN2: Swin 1H 27
St Ambrose Cl. SN3: Swin 2C 30
St Andrews Cl. SN4: Wro 3C 32
St Andrews Ct. SN4: Wro 3C 32
SN25: Blun 4A 12
St Andrews Grn. SN3: Swin 1D 30
ST ANDREW'S RIDGE 4B 12
St Austell Way SN2: Swin 2A 28
St Clements Ct. *SN3: Swin* *4H 29*
(off Horsham Cres.)
St Helens Gdns. SN4: Wro 5C 32
St Helens Vw. SN1: Swin 4A 28
St Ives Ct. SN3: Swin 1B 30
St James Cl. SN2: Stra S 1E 21
St John Rd. SN4: Wro 3B 32
St Josephs Way SN15: Lyne 3F 37
St Julians Cl. SN3: S Mars 2D 22
St Katherine Grn. SN3: Swin 1D 30
St Katherines Pl. SN4: Wan 4F 31
St Margaret Pk. SN3: Stra S 4C 22
St Margarets Grn. SN3: Stra S 4A 22
St Margaret's Rd. SN3: Swin 5E 29
St Mark's Tennis Cen. 6D 20
St Mary's Cl. SN15: Brad 2A 36
St Mary's Gro. SN2: Swin 6C 20
St Michaels Av. SN6: High 4D 8
St Michaels Cl. SN15: Lyne 1D 36
St Paul's Dr. SN3: Swin 1D 30
St Paul's St. SN2: Swin 5D 20
St Philip's Rd. SN2: Stra S 3F 21
Salcombe Gro. SN3: Swin 3G 29
Salisbury St. SN1: Swin 1F 5 (1D 28)
Salop Cl. SN6: Shriv 6E 17
Saltash Rd. SN2: Swin 3A 28
Saltram Cl. SN3: Swin 2B 30
Salt Spring Dr. SN4: Woot B 4B 24
Salzgitter Ct. *SN5: Swin* *3F 27*
(off Affleck Cl.)
Salzgitter Dr. SN25: Swin 4B 12
Sams La. SN26: Blun 2D 12
Sandacre Rd. SN5: Swin 6C 18
SANDALWOOD COURT 2A 22
Sandbourne Rd. SN25: Swin 1G 19
Sanders Cl. SN2: Stra S 1G 21
Sandgate SN3: Stra S 5A 22
Sandgate M. SN3: Stra S 5A 22
Sand Hill SN6: Shriv 5D 16
Sandown Av. SN3: Swin 5F 29
Sandpiper Bri. SN3: Swin 1D 30
Sandringham Rd. SN3: Swin 5G 29
Sandstone Rd. SN25: Swin 5A 12
Sandwood Cl. SN5: Swin 4E 19
Sandy La. SN1: Swin 4C 28
SN6: Shriv 6E 17
Sanford St. SN1: Swin 3E 5 (2D 28)
Sarsen Cl. SN1: Swin 4A 28
Savernake Ct. SN1: Swin 6E 5
Savernake St. SN1: Swin 6D 4 (3D 28)
Savill Cres. SN4: Wro 3A 32
Sawyer Rd. SN25: Swin 6C 12
Saxon Cl. SN6: Crick 3E 7
Saxon Ct. SN3: Swin 4E 29
Saxon Mill SN4: Chi 6C 34
Saxon Orchard SN6: Watch 2G 17
Saxton Wlk. SN5: Swin 6E 19
Scarborough Rd. SN2: Swin 6A 20
Scarlet Cl. SN25: Swin 5A 12
Scholar Cl. SN6: Watch 5H 17
School Cl. SN3: Stra S 3A 22
SN4: Chi 6C 34
School La. SN4: Wro 4B 32
School Row SN25: Swin 2H 19
Science Mus. at Wroughton 6A 32
Scimitar Way SN3: Stra S 1A 22
Scorhill La. SN1: Swin 6B 28
Scotby Av. SN3: Swin 5F 29
Scotney Cres. SN25: Swin 6A 12
Scott Way SN1: Swin 6F 27
Seacole Cres. SN1: Swin 5B 28
Seagry Ct. SN2: Swin 1C 20
Seaton Cl. SN25: Swin 1A 20
Sedgebrook SN3: Swin 6C 30
Sefton Rd. SN25: Swin 5F 11
Selby Cres. SN5: Swin 4E 27
Seldon Cl. SN3: Swin 2F 29
Selwood Cl. SN1: Swin 1F 29
Semley Wlk. SN2: Swin 2D 20
Sevenfields SN6: High 3F 9
SEVENHAMPTON 2G 15
Severn Av. SN25: Swin 2A 20
Seymour Rd. SN3: Swin 2G 29
Shaftesbury Av. SN3: Swin 5A 30
Shaftesbury Cen. SN2: Swin 2A 4
Shaftesbury Cl. SN5: Pur 4C 10
Shakespeare Path SN2: Stra S 3G 21
Shakespeare Rd. SN4: Woot B 2E 25
Shalbourne Cl. SN2: Swin 1C 20
Shanklin Rd. SN25: Swin 2H 19
Shaplands SN3: Stra S 4H 21
Shapwick Cl. SN3: Swin 1B 30
Sharp Cl. SN5: Swin 1E 27
Shaw Ridge Leisure Pk. SN5: Swin 2E 27
Shaw Rd. SN5: Swin 1E 27
(Bankfoot Cl.)
SN5: Swin 2F 27
(The Chesters)
Shaw Village Cen. SN5: Swin 1D 26
Shearings, The SN1: Swin 4D 28
Shearwood Rd. SN5: Swin 5D 18
Sheen Cl. SN5: Swin 4C 26
Sheep St. SN6: High 4F 9
Sheerwold Cl. SN3: Stra S 3A 22
Shelfinch SN5: Swin 4G 27
Shelley Av. SN4: Woot B 2E 25
Shelley St. SN1: Swin 5C 4 (3C 28)
Shenton Cl. SN3: Stra S 3A 22
Shenton Ct. SN3: Stra S 4A 22
Shepherds Breach SN4: Woot B 3D 24
Sheppard St. SN1: Swin 3C 4 (2C 28)
Shepperton Way SN25: Swin 6B 12
(Baxter Cl.)
SN25: Swin 6A 12
(Colbert Pk.)
Sherborne Pl. SN3: Swin 1A 30
Sherfields SN4: Woot B 4E 25
Sherford Rd. SN25: Swin 2H 19
Sheridan Dr. SN4: Woot B 2E 25
Sheringham Ct. *SN3: Swin* *5C 30*
(off Liden Dr.)
Sherston Av. SN2: Swin 1D 20
Sherwood Rd. SN3: Swin 4A 30
Shetland Cl. SN5: Swin 1D 26
Shield Dr. SN15: Lyne 4E 37
Shipley Dr. SN25: Swin 6A 12
Shipton Gro. SN3: Swin 3F 29
Shire Cl. SN5: Swin 1D 26
Shire Ct. SN1: Swin 6A 4 (3B 28)
Shirley Cl. SN3: Swin 1G 29
Short St. SN6: Watch 3G 17
Shoscombe Grn. SN3: Swin 2A 30
Showfield SN4: Woot B 2C 24
Shrewsbury Rd. SN3: Swin 2G 29

Shrewton Wlk. SN2: Swin 6D 12
SHRIVENHAM .6E 17
Shrivenham Hundred Bus. Pk. SN6: Watch . . .2F 17
Shrivenham Rd. SN1: Swin 3H 5 (1F 29)
(not continuous)
SN3: S Mars 4D 22
SN6: High 5F 9
SN6: S Mars 4D 22
Shropshire Cl. SN5: Swin 1E 27
Shute Av. SN6: Watch 4G 17
Sidney Cl. SN3: Swin 2F 29
SN5: Swin 4C 26
Sigerson Rd. SN25: Swin 1F 19
Signal Way SN3: Swin 5E 29
Silbury M. SN25: Swin 3H 19
Silchester Way SN5: Swin 2F 27
Silto Ct. SN2: Swin 5A 20
Silverton Rd. SN3: Swin 2A 30
Simnel Cl. SN5: Swin 3C 26
Siren Cl. SN3: Stra S 6A 22
Skewbridge Cl. SN4: Woot B 4B 24
Skinner's Cl. SN6: Hann 3A 8
Skye Cl. SN6: High 3E 9
Slade Dr. SN3: Stra S 6H 21
(not continuous)
Slade St. SN2: Swin 4H 19
Slate Mdw. SN4: Wan 5G 31
Sleaford Cl. SN5: Swin 2D 26
Slessor Rd. SN15: Lyne 4E 37
Slipper La. SN4: Chi 6C 34
Smart Cl. SN25: Swin 4H 11
Smitan Brook SN3: Swin 2C 30
Smiths Ct. SN5: Pur 4C 10
Snapps Cl. SN4: Wro 5C 32
SNODSHILL RDBT. 5B 30
Snowdon Pl. SN2: Stra S 2F 21
Snowdrop Cl. SN25: Swin 1G 19
Snowshill Cl. SN25: Swin 1A 20
Somerdale Cl. SN2: Swin 2F 27
Somerford Cl. SN2: Swin 2E 21
Somerset Ct. SN4: Wan 5H 31
Somerset Rd. SN2: Swin 5A 20
Somerville Rd. SN3: Swin 2G 29
Sophia Ho. SN3: Swin 6A 22
(off Twickenham Cl.)
Sorrel Cl. SN4: Woot B 1D 24
Sound Copse SN5: Swin 4E 19
Southampton St. SN1: Swin 4G 5 (2E 29)
Southbank Glen SN4: Woot B 3E 25
Southbrook St. SN2: Swin 6C 20
Southbrook St. Extension SN2: Swin 5C 20
Southdown SN4: Wan 6G 31
South Dr. SN25: Blun 4A 12
Southernwood Dr. SN25: Swin 2F 19
Southey Cl. SN25: Swin 4A 12
SOUTH MARSTON 1D 22
Sth. Marston Ind. Est. SN3: S Mars 6B 14
South Mdw. La. SN6: Pur S 1B 10
SN26: Pur S 1B 10
South St. SN1: Swin 6F 5 (4D 28)
SN6: Watch 3G 17
Southview SN15: Lyne 1E 37
South Vw. Av. SN3: Swin 3F 29
Southwick Av. SN2: Swin 1C 20
Southwold Cl. SN1: Swin 6E 11
Soyuz Cres. SN25: Swin 5E 11
Spa Cl. SN6: High 4G 9
SPARCELLS .4E 19
Sparcells Dr. SN5: Swin 4E 19
Sparrows La. SN4: Woot B 3C 24
Speedwell Cl. SN25: Swin 1H 19
Spencer Cl. SN5: Swin 1C 26
Spencers Orchard SN4: Wro 4B 32
Spenser Cl. SN3: Swin 1H 29
Speresholt SN5: Swin 1A 20
Spindle Tree Ct. SN2: Swin 4C 20
Spinney Cl. SN4: Lidd 3G 35
Spital La. SN6: Crick 3F 7
Spitfire Way SN3: S Mars 5B 14
SPITTLEBOROUGH RDBT. 6B 26
Spode Cl. SN25: Swin 5G 11
Sprats Barn Cres. SN4: Woot B 3E 25
Spring Cl. SN1: Swin 3F 5 (2D 28)
Springfield Cl. SN6: Shriv 6E 17
Springfield Cres. SN4: Woot B 3C 24
Springfield Rd. SN1: Swin 3D 28
Spring Gdns. SN1: Swin 4F 5 (2D 28)
SPRING GARDENS RDBT. 3F 5 (2D 28)
Springhill Cl. SN5: Swin 3F 27
Springlines SN4: Wan 5H 31
Spruce Ct. SN2: Swin 4C 20
(off Tree Courts Rd.)
Spur Way SN2: Stra S 3F 21
Square, The SN1: Swin 4E 29
Squires Copse SN5: Swin 5D 18
Squires Ct. SN6: High 5E 9
Squires Hill Cl. SN4: Woot B 3E 25
Squires Rd. SN6: Watch 3G 17

Squirrel Cres. SN4: Woot B 3E 25
Stable Ct. SN4: Woot B 3C 24
Stacey's La. SN4: Wan 6H 31
Stackpole Cres. SN25: Swin 4F 11
Stafford St. SN1: Swin 6D 4 (3C 28)
Stainswick La. SN6: Shriv 6F 17
Staldon Rd. SN1: Swin 6C 28
Stalldown Rd. SN1: Swin 6B 28
Stallpits La. SN6: Shriv 5C 16
Stallpits Rd. SN6: Shriv 5D 16
Stamford St. SN3: Swin 3E 27
Stannon La. SN1: Swin 6C 28
Stancombe Pk. SN5: Swin 3G 27
Standen Way SN5: Swin 5B 12
Standings Cl. SN5: Swin 6D 18
Stanford Rd. SN25: Swin 5F 11
Stanier St. SN1: Swin 5D 4 (3C 28)
Stanley Cl. SN4: Wan 5G 31
Stanley Honey Ct. SN3: Swin 2G 29
Stanley St. SN1: Swin 6F 5 (3D 28)
Stanmore St. SN1: Swin 6B 4 (3B 28)
Stannon La. SN1: Swin 6C 28
Stansfield Cl. SN5: Swin 4G 27
Stanton Cl. SN3: S Mars 5B 14
STANTON FITZWARREN 2A 14
Stanway Cl. SN5: Swin 4H 29
Stapleford Cl. SN2: Swin 6C 12
Stapleford Way SN2: Swin 6C 12
Stapler's La. SN6: Hann 5A 8
Stapleton Cl. SN6: High 5E 9
Stardust Cres. SN25: Swin 5D 10
Staring Cl. SN5: Swin 6C 18
Star La. SN6: Watch 3F 17
Star West SN5: Swin 1G 27
Station App. SN1: Swin 5E 29
Station Halt SN3: Stra S 4B 22
Station Ind. Est. SN1: Swin 3C 4 (2C 28)
Station Rd. SN1: Swin 2D 4 (1C 28)
SN4: Chi 6C 34
SN4: Woot B 4C 24
SN5: Pur, Wid 5C 10
SN6: High 4E 9
SN6: Shriv 6E 17
Station Yd. SN5: Wid 4C 10
Staverton Way SN5: Swin 6D 12
Steadings, The SN4: Woot B 4E 25
STEAM Mus. of the Great Western Railway
. . . . .3B 4 (2B 28)
Stedham Wlk. SN3: Swin 4A 30
Steeple Vw. SN1: Swin 4E 29
Stenbury Cl. SN25: Swin 5B 12
Stenness Cl. SN5: Swin 4F 19
Stephenson Rd. SN25: Swin 5D 12
Stephens Rd. SN3: Stra S 5H 21
Stevenson Rd. SN25: Swin 1F 19
Stewart Cl. SN25: Swin 6C 12
Stinsford Cres. SN25: Swin 6F 11
Stirling Cl. SN4: Wro 3B 32
Stirling Rd. SN3: S Mars 6B 14
Stockbridge Copse SN5: Swin 4E 19
Stockham Cl. SN6: Crick 2F 7
Stockham Gdns. SN6: Crick 2F 7
Stockton Rd. SN2: Swin 2D 20
Stoke Comn. La. SN5: Pur S 2A 10
Stokesay Dr. SN5: Swin 4F 27
Stonecrop Way SN25: Swin 1H 19
Stonefield Cl. SN5: Swin 1F 27
SN6: Shriv 6F 17
Stonefield Dr. SN6: High 6F 9
Stonehenge Rd. SN1: Swin 6B 28
Stonehill Grn. SN5: Swin 2G 27
Stonehurst Cl. SN3: Stra S 5H 21
Stone La. SN5: Lyd M 6A 18
Stoneover La. SN4: Woot B 3E 25
Stones La. SN6: Crick 1B 6
Stoneybeck Cl. SN25: Swin 2G 27
Stour Rd. SN25: Swin 2C 20
Stour Wlk. SN25: Swin 2C 20
Stranks Cl. SN6: High 6F 9
Stratford Cl. SN3: Swin 3H 21
Stratton Ct. SN3: Stra S 3H 21
SN5: Pur 5B 10
STRATTON GREEN 5A 22
Stratton Orchard SN3: Stra S 4H 21
Stratton Rd. SN1: Swin 6G 11
SN2: Swin 6G 11
STRATTON ST MARGARET 3A 22
Stratton St Margaret By-Pass SN3: Stra S . . .1H 21
SN3: Swin 6D 30
SN25: Swin 5E 13
Street, The SN4: Lidd 3G 35
SN5: Lyd M 6A 18
SN25: Swin 6B 10
(not continuous)
Stroma Way SN6: High 3D 8
Strouds Cl. SN3: Swin 5E 29
Stroud's Hill SN4: Chi 6C 34
Stuart Cl. SN3: Swin 2G 29

Stubsmead SN3: Swin 3B 30
Studio, The SN1: Swin 4G 5
Studland Cl. SN3: Swin 5A 30
Sudeley Way SN5: Swin 3C 26
Suffolk St. SN2: Swin 6D 20
Summerhouse Rd. SN4: Wro 3A 32
Summers St. SN2: Swin 1A 4 (1A 28)
Sunflowers, The SN2: Stra S 3E 21
Sun La. SN4: Wro 5B 32
Sunningdale Rd. SN25: Swin 2D 20
Sunnyside Av. SN1: Swin 6A 4 (4B 28)
Supermarine Rd. SN3: S Mars 4C 14
Supermarine Rugby Club 4C 14
Surrey Rd. SN2: Swin 5B 20
Sussex Sq. SN1: Swin 2G 29
Sutton Pk. SN26: Blun 3D 12
Sutton Rd. SN3: Swin 4B 30
Swallowdale SN3: Swin 1C 30
Swallowfield Av. SN3: Swin 3G 29
Swallows Mead SN4: Woot B 3F 25
Swanage Wlk. SN25: Swin 3H 19
SWANBOROUGH 6B 8
Swanbrook SN3: Swin 6C 22
Swan Cl. SN3: Stra S 6A 22
Swift Av. SN25: Swin 5B 12
Swinburne Pl. SN4: Woot B 2D 24
SWINDON 4D 4 (2C 28)
Swindon & Cricklade Railway
Hayes Knoll Station 2C 10
Taw Valley Halt Station 1E 10
Swindon Bus Station 2E 5 (1D 28)
Swindon Europark SN5: Swin 6E 27
Swindon Mus. & Art Gallery 4D 28
(off Bath Rd.)
SWINDON NEW TOWN 4E 5 (2D 28)
Swindon Rd. SN1: Swin 6E 5 (3D 28)
SN3: Stan F 4C 14
SN3: Stra S 5H 21
SN4: Woot B 1E 25
SN4: Wro 3C 32
SN6: Calc, Crick 3G 7
SN6: High, Stan F 4C 14
Swindon Stadium (Greyhound & Speedway)
. . . . .4B 12
Swindon Station (Rail) 2D 4 (1C 28)
Swindon St. SN6: High 5F 9
Swindon Supermarine FC 4C 14
Swindon Town FC 2H 5 (1E 29)
Swinley Dr. SN5: Swin 4D 18
Sword Gdns. SN5: Swin 4A 28
Sycamore Cl. SN15: Lyne 3G 37
Sycamore Gro. SN2: Swin 4D 20
Symonds SN5: Swin 5E 27
Syon Cl. SN3: Swin 6A 12
Sywell Rd. SN3: Stra S 6B 22

T

Tadpole La. SN25: Blun 4D 10
Tallis Wlk. SN5: Swin 3D 26
Tallow La. SN4: Wan 5G 31
Tamar Cl. SN25: Swin 2B 20
Tamworth Dr. SN5: Swin 1D 26
Tanners Cl. SN4: Woot B 3C 24
Tansley Moor SN25: Swin 5D 30
Taplow Wlk. SN3: Swin 4H 29
Tarka Cl. SN25: Swin 5A 12
Tarragon Cl. SN2: Swin 2F 19
Tatley Wlk. SN4: Chi 6D 34
Tatry Rd. SN25: Swin 6G 11
Tattershall SN5: Swin 5F 27
Taunton St. SN1: Swin 4B 4 (2B 28)
Tavistock Rd. SN3: Swin 2A 30
TAW HILL 1F 19
Tawny Owl Cl. SN3: Stra S 6B 22
Taw Valley Halt Station
Swindon & Cricklade Railway 1E 19
Taylor Cres. SN3: Stra S 2H 21
Teal Av. SN15: Lyne 3E 37
Tealsbrook SN3: Swin 1C 30
Techno Trad. Est. SN2: Swin 5F 21
(Athena Av.)
SN2: Swin 5F 21
(Bramble Rd.)
Tedder Cl. SN2: Swin 4C 20
Tees Cl. SN25: Swin 2B 20
Teeswater Cl. SN5: Swin 2D 26
Telford Pool SN2: Swin 6A 20
Telford Way SN5: Swin 4G 27
Templars Firs SN4: Woot B 5D 24
Templar's Way Ind. Est. SN4: Woot B 6C 24
Temple St. SN1: Swin 5E 5 (3D 28)
Tenby Cl. SN3: Swin 5G 29
Tennyson Rd. SN4: Woot B 3C 24
Tennyson St. SN1: Swin 5C 4 (3C 28)
Tenpin Bowling 2E 27
Tenzing Gdns. SN25: Swin 3D 20

Terncliff SN3: Swin 1C 30
TESTHOUSE RDBT. 2A 4 (1B 28)
TEWKESBURY CROSS RDBT. 2E 27
Tewkesbury Way SN5: Swin 1B 26
Thackeray Cl. SN3: Swin 4C 30
Thames Av. SN25: Swin 1H 19
Thames Cl. SN6: Crick 2F 7
        (off Thames La.)
Thamesdown Dr. SN2: Swin 6F 11
  SN25: Swin 6F 11
Thames La. SN6: Crick 2F 7
Thames Path SN6: Ash K 1A 6
  SN6: Crick .2F 7
Thatchers, The SN25: Swin 5D 12
The . . . .
    Names prefixed with 'The' for example
    'The Acorns' are indexed under the main
    name such as 'Acorns, The'
Theatre Sq. SN1: Swin 5F 5
Theobald St. SN1: Swin 4C 4 (2C 28)
Thetford Way SN25: Swin 1F 19
Thirlmere SN3: Swin 5D 30
Thistledown SN4: Wan 5G 31
Thistly Mead RDBT. 1F 21
Thomas Edward Coard Bldg. SN2: Swin 6E 21
    (off Cricklade Rd.)
Thomas St. SN2: Swin 1A 4 (1A 28)
Thompson Ct. SN5: Pur 6A 10
Thorley Ct. SN25: Swin 6B 12
Thornbridge Av. SN3: Swin 4H 29
Thorne Rd. SN3: Swin 4B 30
Thornford Dr. SN5: Swin 3F 27
Thornhill Dr. SN25: Swin 4A 12
Thornhill Ind. Est. SN3: S Mars 3C 22
Thornhill Rd. SN3: S Mars 4C 22
Three Sisters Rd. SN4: Wan 5H 31
Thresher Dr. SN25: Swin 5D 12
Thrushel Cl. SN25: Swin 2H 19
Thurlestone Rd. SN3: Swin 3F 29
Thurney Dr. SN5: Swin 4C 26
Thursday St. SN25: Swin 6F 11
Thyme Cl. SN2: Swin 3F 19
Tidworth Cl. SN5: Swin 4A 28
Tilley's La. SN3: Stra S 5H 21
Tilshead Wlk. SN2: Swin 1C 20
Timandra Cl. SN25: Swin 6B 12
Timony Pl. SN1: Swin 1C 32
Tinkers Fld. SN4: Woot B 3C 24
Tintagel Cl. SN5: Swin 4E 27
Tippett Av. SN25: Swin 5H 11
Tisbury Cl. SN2: Swin 6D 12
Tismeads Cres. SN1: Swin 6D 28
Titchfield Cl. SN3: Swin 3C 26
Tithe Barn Cres. SN1: Swin 4A 28
Tiverton Rd. SN2: Swin 5D 20
TOCKENHAM .2H 37
Tockenham Way SN2: Swin 6C 12
Tollard Cl. SN3: Swin 2B 30
TOOTHILL 4F 27
TOOTHILL RDBT. 3E 27
Toppers Cl. SN25: Swin 3B 20
Torridge Cl. SN25: Swin 2A 20
Torrington Ct. SN3: Swin 3H 29
    (off Welcombe Av.)
Tortworth Rd. SN25: Swin 5F 11
Torun Way SN2: Swin 1G 19
  SN25: Swin 6G 11
Totterdown Cl. SN3: Swin 1D 30
Tourist Info. Cen.
  Cricklade 2F 7
  Swindon 5F 5 (3D 28)
Tovey Rd. SN2: Swin 4B 20
Towcester Rd. SN3: Stra S 6B 22
Tower Rd. SN5: Swin 4E 19
Townsend Rd. SN6: Shriv 6D 16
Towpath Gdns. SN1: Swin 6A 4
Tracy Cl. SN25: Swin 6B 12
Trajan Rd. SN3: Stra S 5B 22
Transfer Bri. Ind. Est. SN1: Swin . . .1H 5 (6E 21)
TRANSFER BRIDGES RDBT. 1G 5 (6E 21)
Trecastle Rd. SN1: Swin 6B 28
Tree Courts Rd. SN2: Swin 4C 20
Treforest Cl. SN25: Swin 5F 11
Tregantle Wlk. SN3: Swin 2B 30
Tregoze Way SN5: Swin 2C 26
Trenchard Rd. SN6: Stan F 2A 14
  SN15: Lyne 4E 37
Trentham Cl. SN3: Swin 4H 29
Trent Rd. SN25: Swin 2B 20
Trevello Rd. SN3: Swin 6C 28
Tricentre SN1: Swin 3E 5
Trinity Cl. SN3: Swin 5H 29
Trinity Ho. SN3: Swin 5H 29
Trowbridge Cl. SN3: Swin 2E 21
Truman Cl. SN3: Swin 4B 30
Truro Path SN5: Swin 4F 27
Truscott Av. SN25: Swin 5H 11
Tryon Cl. SN3: Swin 6C 30

Tudor Cres. SN3: Stra S 5A 22
Tudor Wlk. SN3: Swin 2G 29
Tuke Wlk. SN1: Swin 5B 28
Tulip Tree Cl. SN2: Swin 4D 20
Turl St. SN1: Swin 3F 5 (2D 28)
Turnball SN4: Chi 6C 34
Turnball M. SN4: Chi 6C 34
    (off Turnball)
Turncliffe SN3: Swin 6F 29
Turner St. SN1: Swin 6A 4 (3B 28)
Turnham Grn. SN25: Swin 5E 27
Turnpike Rd. SN6: High 4F 9
  SN26: Blun 4C 12
Tuscan Ct. SN25: Swin 5G 11
Tweed Cl. SN25: Swin 2A 20
Twelve Oaks Golf Course 1E 9
Twickenham Cl. SN25: Swin 6A 22
Twineham Rd. SN25: Swin 4E 11
Twyford Cl. SN3: Swin 2H 29
Tyburn Cl. SN5: Swin 3E 27
Tydeman St. SN2: Swin 5E 21
Tye Gdns. SN5: Swin 3C 26
Tyndale Path SN5: Swin 3D 26
Tyndale Gdns. SN3: Swin 2B 30
Tyneham Rd. SN3: Swin 2B 30

U

Ullswater Cl. SN3: Swin 5D 30
Ulysses Rd. SN25: Swin 5E 11
Underdown Cl. SN4: Wan 5G 31
Union Row SN1: Swin 4E 29
Union St. SN1: Swin 6F 5 (3D 28)
Upavon Ct. SN2: Swin 1D 20
Upfield SN3: Swin 1D 20
Upham Rd. SN3: Swin 6H 5 (3E 29)
Upper Pavenhill SN5: Pur 5A 10
UPPER STRATTON 2F 21
UPPER WANBOROUGH 6G 31
Upton Cl. SN25: Swin 1A 20
Urchfont Way SN2: Swin 2D 20
Ursa Way SN25: Swin 5E 11
Utah Cl. SN5: Swin 4A 28
Uxbridge Rd. SN5: Swin 5D 26

V

Vale Vw. SN4: Woot B 4C 24
Valleyside SN1: Swin 4B 28
Vanbrugh Ga. SN3: Swin 1G 33
Vasterne Cl. SN5: Pur 5B 10
Vastern Wharf SN4: Woot B 5A 24
Vaughan Williams Way SN25: Swin 5G 11
Vega Cl. SN25: Swin 5E 11
Ventnor Cl. SN25: Swin 2H 19
Verney Cl. SN3: Swin 2C 30
Verulam Cl. SN3: Stra S 6C 22
Verwood Cl. SN3: Swin 3H 29
Vespasian Cl. SN3: Stra S 6B 22
Vicarage La. SN6: High 4F 9
  SN6: Shriv 6F 17
Vicarage Rd. SN2: Swin 5A 20
Vicarage Vw. SN1: Swin 6G 5
Victoria Cl. SN11: New Z 5C 36
Victoria Ct. SN5: Swin 4F 27
Victoria Cross Rd. SN4: Wro 3A 32
Victoria Dr. SN15: Lyne 4G 37
Victoria Rd. SN1: Swin 5F 5 (3D 28)
Victory Row SN4: Woot B 3C 24
Viking Cl. SN25: Swin 5A 12
Village Grn. SN5: Swin 4F 27
Villett St. SN1: Swin 4C 4 (2C 28)
Villiers Cl. SN5: Swin 1C 26
Viscount Way SN3: S Mars 6B 14
Vistula Cres. SN25: Swin 6H 11
Volpe Cl. SN5: Swin 4C 26
Volta Rd. SN1: Swin 3F 5 (2D 28)
Vorda Rd. SN6: High 3F 9
Vowley Vw. SN4: Woot B 4E 25
Voyager Dr. SN25: Swin 5E 11

W

Wade Rd. SN25: Swin 5G 11
Waggoner Cl. SN3: Swin 6C 12
Wagtail Cl. SN3: Stra S 6B 22
Wainwright Cl. SN3: Swin 4C 30
Wainwright M. SN4: Wro 4C 32
Waite Meads Cl. SN5: Pur 5C 10
Wakefield Cl. SN5: Swin 4D 26
WALCOT EAST .3H 29
Walcot Rd. SN3: Swin 5H 5 (3E 29)
WALCOT WEST .3F 29
Waldron Cl. SN3: Swin 4B 30
Walkinshaw Rd. SN2: Swin 4H 19

Wallingford Cl. SN5: Swin 5F 27
Wallis Dr. SN25: Swin 4B 12
Wallsworth Rd. SN3: Swin 4H 29
Walnut Cl. SN3: Swin 4F 21
Walnut Tree Cl. SN3: Stra S 3A 22
Walnut Tree Gdns. SN5: Lyd M 6A 18
Walsingham Rd. SN3: Swin 2G 29
Walter Cl. SN5: Swin 2D 26
Walton Cl. SN3: Swin 4G 29
Walton Grange SN1: Swin 4D 28
Walwayne Fld. SN3: Stra S 1H 21
WANBOROUGH .5H 31
Wanborough Rd. SN3: Stra S 5B 22
  SN3: Wan 1E 31
  SN4: Wan 1E 31
Wanshot Cl. SN4: Wro 5D 32
Warbeck Ga. SN5: Swin 3C 26
Wardley Cl. SN3: Swin 4H 29
Wardour Cl. SN5: Swin 5F 29
Wareham Cl. SN5: Swin 3E 27
Warminster Av. SN2: Swin 1D 20
Warneage Grn. SN4: Wan 6G 31
Warneford Cl. SN5: Swin 4G 27
Warner Cl. SN3: Stra S 3A 22
Warrener Cl. SN25: Swin 5C 12
Warwick Ho. SN3: Swin 3C 30
Warwick Rd. SN1: Swin 6E 5 (3D 28)
Washbourne Rd. SN4: Woot B 4D 24
WASHPOOL 5C 18
WATCHFIELD 3G 17
WATCHFIELD RDBT. 2H 17
Watercrook M. SN5: Swin 3G 27
Waterdown Cl. SN25: Swin 2F 19
Water Fld. SN5: Pur 6A 10
Water Furlongs SN6: Crick 3E 7
Watermead SN3: Stra S 4B 22
Waterside Way SN3: Swin 1C 34
Watery La. SN5: Swin 1C 26
Watling Cl. SN2: Swin 2H 27
Wavell Rd. SN2: Swin 4C 20
Waverley Rd. SN3: Stra S 5B 22
Waylands SN6: Crick 3F 7
Wayne Cl. SN3: Swin 1B 20
Wayside Cl. SN2: Swin 1H 27
Wayte St. SN2: Swin 3H 19
Weavers, The SN3: Swin 4E 29
Webbs Cl. SN15: Lyne 2E 37
Webbs Wood SN5: Swin 4D 18
Webbs Wood Stadium 4C 18
Wedgewood Cl. SN2: Swin 1A 4 (1B 28)
Weedon Rd. SN3: Stra S 6A 22
Weirside Av. SN4: Wro 4C 32
Welbeck Cl. SN3: Swin 3G 29
Welford Cl. SN3: Stra S 6B 22
Well Cl. SN4: Chi 6C 34
Wellington Rd. SN3: S Mars 6B 14
Wellington Sq. SN6: Watch 3G 17
Wellington St. SN1: Swin 2E 5 (1D 28)
Wells St. SN1: Swin 4F 5 (3D 28)
Welton Rd. SN5: Swin 2G 27
Wembley St. SN2: Swin 6A 20
Wensleydale Cl. SN5: Swin 2E 27
Wentworth Pk. SN5: Swin 4D 26
    (not continuous)
Wesley Ct. SN4: Woot B 2E 25
Wesley St. SN1: Swin 4D 28
Wessex Cl. SN1: Swin 5F 5
Wessex Way SN6: High 3G 9
Westbourne Ct. SN2: Swin 2A 28
Westbrook Rd. SN2: Swin 5B 20
Westbury Pk. SN4: Woot B 4C 24
Westbury Rd. SN2: Swin 1C 20
Westcott Pl. SN1: Swin 6A 4 (3B 28)
Westcott St. SN1: Swin 5A 4 (3B 28)
West Dr. SN25: Blun 4A 12
West End Rd. SN3: Stra S 5H 21
  SN6: Shriv 6D 16
Western St. SN1: Swin 6F 5 (3D 28)
Westfield Way SN2: Swin 2G 19
  SN25: Swin 2G 19
W. Highland Rd. SN25: Swin 5A 12
West Hill SN6: Blun 2C 12
Westhill Cl. SN6: High 5E 9
WESTLEA 3F 27
Westlea Campus SN5: Swin 3F 27
Westlea Dr. SN5: Swin 3F 27
WESTLEA RDBT. .2G 27
Westlecot Ho. SN1: Swin 5C 28
Westlecot Indoor Bowls Club 5D 28
Westlecot Rd. SN1: Swin 5C 28
WESTMEAD 1G 27
Westmead Dr. SN5: Swin 1G 27
Westmead Ind. Est. SN5: Swin 2G 27
WESTMEAD RDBT. 1G 27
West Mill La. SN6: Crick 2D 6
Westminster Rd. SN5: Swin 4E 27
Westmorland Rd. SN1: Swin 5G 5 (3E 29)

WESTROP 4E 9
Westrop SN6: High 4F 9
W. Swindon Cen. SN5: Swin 3E 27
WEST TOCKENHAM 2H 37
West Vw. SN3: Swin 1A 30
Westwood Rd. SN2: Swin 6D 12
Wey Cl. SN25: Swin 2B 20
Weyhill Cl. SN3: Swin 3H 29
Whalley Cres. SN4: Wro 4A 32
Wharf Rd. SN4: Wro 2A 32
Wharncliffe St. SN25: Swin 4G 11
Wheatcroft Way SN1: Swin 6F 21
Wheatlands SN25: Swin 2H 19
Wheatstone Rd. SN3: Swin 4D 30
Wheeler Av. SN2: Swin 3E 21
Whilestone Way SN3: Stra S 5B 22
Whitbourne Av. SN3: Swin 3G 29
Whitbred Cl. SN5: Swin 1E 27
Whitby Gro. SN2: Swin 5A 20
Whitcombe Cl. SN15: Lyne 5D 36
White Beam Ct. SN2: Swin 4C 20
White Castle SN5: Swin 5F 27
White Eagle Rd. SN25: Swin 1G 19
(not continuous)
White Edge Moor SN3: Swin 5D 30
Whitefield Cres. SN5: Swin 5D 18
WHITE HART RDBT. 4C 22
Whitehead St. SN1: Swin 5C 4 (3C 28)
Whitehill Ind. Est. SN4: Woot B 4A 24
Whitehill La. SN4: Woot B 3A 24
Whitehill Way SN5: Swin 5C 26
White Horse Rd. SN6: Crick 2E 7
Whitehouse Rd. SN2: Swin . . .1E 5 (6C 20)
(not continuous)
Whitelands Rd. SN3: Stra S 5H 21
Whiteman St. SN2: Swin 6D 20
Whitethorn Cl. SN4: Woot B 1D 24
Whitgift Cl. SN5: Swin 2C 26
Whitmore Cl. SN5: Swin 2C 26
Whitney St. SN1: Swin 5E 5 (3D 28)
Whittingham Dr. SN4: Wro 6H 33
Whittington Rd. SN5: Swin 2F 27
Whitworth Rd. SN3: Swin 3B 20
Wichelstok Cl. SN1: Swin 5D 28
WICHELSTOWE 6C 28
Wickdown Av. SN25: Swin 3A 20
Wick La. SN3: Swin 6D 30
(not continuous)
SN3: Wan .2E 31
Wicks Cl. SN25: Swin 1H 19
WIDHAM 4C 10
Widhill La. SN26: Blun 3B 12
Wigmore Av. SN3: Swin 4G 29
Wilcot Av. SN2: Swin 1E 21
Wilcox Cl. SN3: Swin 4D 20
Wild Acre SN4: Wan 5G 31
Wildern Sq. SN3: Stra S 2H 21
Wilkins Cl. SN3: Stra S 1G 21
William Robbins Ct. SN25: Swin 3H 19
William St. SN1: Swin 6A 4 (3B 28)
Willington Rd. SN25: Swin 5H 11
Willis Way SN5: Pur 6B 10
Willmott's Cvn. Pk. SN15: Lyne 1D 36

Willowbrook SN5: Pur 5C 10
Willowherb Cl. SN25: Swin 1H 19
Willows, The SN5: Swin 4D 18
SN6: High .5F 9
Willows Av. SN2: Swin 3D 20
Willow Wlk. SN4: Wro 5C 32
Wills Av. SN1: Swin 6F 21
Wilmot Cl. SN5: Swin 2C 26
Wilsford Ct. SN2: Swin 1D 20
(off Everleigh Rd.)
Wilson Rd. SN25: Swin 6A 12
Wilton Wlk. SN2: Swin 6D 12
Wiltshire Av. SN2: Swin 6B 20
Wiltshire Ct. SN1: Swin 4D 4
(off Farnsby St.)
Wiltshire Cres. SN4: Woot B 6A 24
Wiltshire Ho. SN1: Swin 1G 29
Wimpole Cl. SN3: Swin 4H 29
Winchcombe Cl. SN5: Swin 1C 26
Winchester Cl. SN3: Stra S 5A 22
Windbrook Mdw. SN3: Stra S 2H 21
Windermere SN3: Swin 5D 30
Windflower Rd. SN25: Swin 1H 19
Windmill Cl. SN5: Swin 5D 26
Windmill Hill Bus. Pk. SN5: Swin 5B 26
Windmill Piece SN4: Chi 6C 34
Windmill Rd. SN4: Woot B 4E 25
WINDMILL RDBT. 4C 26
Windrush SN6: High 4E 9
Windrush Rd. SN25: Swin 3B 20
Windsor Rd. SN3: Swin 6F 29
Wingate Pde. SN2: Swin 4B 20
Wingfield SN3: Stra S 1H 21
Wingfield Av. SN2: Swin 6D 12
Winifred St. SN3: Swin 5E 29
Winlaw Cl. SN5: Swin 1F 27
Winsley Cl. SN2: Swin 1D 20
Winstanley Cl. SN5: Swin 4D 26
Winterbourne Rd. SN25: Swin 1G 19
Winterslow Rd. SN2: Swin 1C 20
Winton Rd. SN3: Stra S 2A 22
Winwick Rd. SN5: Swin 4E 27
Wirral Way SN25: Swin 5A 12
Wise Cl. SN2: Stra S 3F 21
Wiseman Cl. SN3: Swin 2D 30
Witfield Cl. SN5: Pur 4B 10
Witham Way SN2: Stra S 2G 21
Withering Rd. SN1: Swin 5B 28
Witheys, The SN4: Wan 5G 31
Withy Cl. SN4: Woot B 2C 24
WITHY MEAD RDBT. 1F 27
Witts La. SN5: Pur 4B 10
Woburn Cl. SN25: Swin 6A 12
Wolsely Av. SN3: Swin 4G 29
Woodbine Ter. SN3: Swin 6B 30
Woodbury Cl. SN5: Swin 6D 18
Woodchester SN5: Swin 3F 27
Woodcutters M. SN5: Swin 6D 12
Woodford Cl. SN2: Swin 6D 12
Wood Hall Dr. SN2: Swin 3G 19
WOOD HALL PARK 2F 19
WOODHALL PARK RDBT. 2F 19
Woodhouse Rd. SN3: Swin 3G 29

Woodland Vw. SN4: Wro 1C 32
WOODSHAW 3F 25
Woodshaw Mead SN4: Woot B 3F 25
Woodside Av. SN3: Swin 3F 29
Woodside Rd. SN3: S Mars 5B 14
Woodsman Rd. SN25: Swin 6C 12
Woodspring Ct. SN1: Swin 5D 28
Woodstock Rd. SN3: Stra S 5B 22
Wood St. SN1: Swin 4E 29
SN4: Wro .3C 24
Woolford Grange SN4: Woot B 3F 25
Woollaton Cl. SN5: Swin 3D 26
Wootton Bassett Rd. SN1: Swin 6A 4 (3H 27)
SN5: Swin 3H 27
WOOTTON BASSETT, ROYAL 3C 24
Wordsworth Cl. SN4: Woot B 2E 25
Wordsworth Dr. SN2: Stra S 2G 21
Worlidge Dr. SN5: Swin 1E 27
Worsley Rd. SN5: Swin 4D 26
Worthington Cl. SN3: Swin 1A 30
Wrag Barn Golf Club 2F 15
Wrde Hill SN6: High 5E 9
Wrenswood SN3: Swin 6C 22
Wright Cl. SN25: Swin 4B 12
WROUGHTON 5B 32
Wroughton (Park & Ride) 1D 32
Wroughton Bus. Pk. SN4: Wro 2D 32
Wyld Ct. SN25: Blun 4H 11
Wylye Cl. SN25: Swin 2A 20
Wyndham Rd. SN2: Swin 1A 4 (6A 20)
Wynndale Cl. SN3: Stra S 2H 21
Wynwards Rd. SN25: Swin 6B 12
Wyvern Cl. SN1: Swin 6D 28
Wyvern Theatre 4F 5 (2D 28)

Y

Yardlee Wlk. SN1: Swin 6B 28
Yardley Cl. SN2: Swin 4A 20
Yarmouth Cl. SN5: Swin 4E 27
Yarnton Cl. SN5: Swin 6D 18
Yarrow Cl. SN2: Swin 3F 19
Yeats Cl. SN25: Swin 4B 12
Yelland Wlk. SN1: Swin 1C 32
Yellowhammer Cl. SN3: Stra S 6B 22
Yeoman Cl. SN5: Swin 1D 26
Yeomans Way SN4: Lidd 3G 35
Yeovil Cl. SN3: Swin 3A 30
Yersin Ct. SN1: Swin 4B 28
Yew Tree Gdns. SN3: S Mars 2D 22
Yiewsley Cres. SN3: Stra S 4A 22
Yonder Way SN4: Wan 5G 31
York Ho. SN3: Swin 3C 30
York Rd. SN1: Swin 5G 5 (3E 29)
SN15: Lyne 3F 37
Youghal Cl. SN6: Shriv 6E 17

Z

Zakopane Rd. SN25: Swin 6G 11
Zoar Cl. SN4: Wro 4B 32

SAFETY CAMERA INFORMATION

PocketGPSWorld.com's CamerAlert is a self-contained speed and red light camera warning system for SatNavs and Android or Apple iOS smartphones/tablets. Visit www.cameralert.com to download.

Safety camera locations are publicised by the Safer Roads Partnership which operates them in order to encourage drivers to comply with speed limits at these sites. It is the driver's absolute responsibility to be aware of and to adhere to speed limits at all times.

By showing this safety camera information it is the intention of Geographers' A-Z Map Company Ltd. to encourage safe driving and greater awareness of speed limits and vehicle speed. Data accurate at time of printing.

Printed and bound in the United Kingdom by Gemini Press Ltd., Shoreham-by-Sea, West Sussex
Printed on materials from a sustainable source